NEW ORLEANS:
FACTS AND LEGENDS

NEW ORLEANS: FACTS AND LEGENDS

by

RAYMOND J. MARTINEZ

AND

JACK D. L. HOLMES

Original Edition

QUID PRO BOOKS
New Orleans, Louisiana

Originally published in 1960 by Hope Publications, Jefferson, Louisiana. No copyright is currently claimed in the contents, depictions, or tables in this book. Modern compilation and facsimile design copyright © 2014 by Steven Alan Childress. All rights reserved.

Published in the 2014 edition by Quaint Press, an imprint of Quid Pro Books. This is an unabridged, facsimile republication of the original 1960 First Edition (in content similar to later printings of the work produced by Hope Publications, such as the 1970 edition). This is a *Digitally Remastered Book*™ by Quid Pro Books.

ISBN 978-1-61027-243-8 (pbk)
ISBN 978-1-61027-247-6 (ebk)

QUID PRO BOOKS
5860 Citrus Blvd.
Suite D-101
New Orleans, Louisiana 70123
www.quaintpress.com

qp

Cover photograph by Jack D. L. Holmes.

ALSO BY QUAINT PRESS AND QUID PRO BOOKS,
IN NEW PRINT AND eBOOK EDITIONS:

*Mysterious Marie Laveau, Voodoo Queen,
And Folk Tales Along The Mississippi*
By Raymond J. Martinez

*Frenchmen, Desire, Good Children
. . . and Other Streets of New Orleans*
By John Churchill Chase

*Louisiana's Fabulous Foods and How to Cook Them: Original Recipes of
Many Louisiana Hostesses and Famous New Orleans' Restaurants*
By Lady Helen Henriques Hardy and Raymond J. Martinez

Clearing the Thickets: A History of Antebellum Alabama
By Herbert James Lewis

Twelve Years a Slave
By Solomon Northup

NEW ORLEANS: FACTS and LEGENDS

By

RAYMOND J. MARTINEZ
Author of Marie Laveau, Voodoo Queen;
Steamboat Days on the Mississippi;
Pierre George Rousseau;
Louisiana's Fabulous Foods
and others.

and

JACK D. L. HOLMES
Author of Gayoso, The Life of a
Spanish Governor in the Mississippi
Valley; Honor and Fidelity;
Louisiana Collection Series
and others.

Photograph on cover by
JACK D. L. HOLMES

HOPE PUBLICATIONS
P. O. BOX 10062
JEFFERSON, LA. 70181

Printed in U.S.A.
by Laborde Printing Co., N. O., La.

Court House (Cabildo), Jackson Square, Putting up the Chain Barrier while Court is in Session. Emblem of the State of Louisiana (the Pelican) over the door of the Old Armory, Near Jackson Square. Old Balcony on Royal Street. A glimpse of a Court Yard. By W. A. Rogers, appearing in HARPER'S WEEKLY for Dec. 30, 1899.

CONTENTS

A Brief History of Mardi Gras 1

Mardi Gras in New Orleans in 1879 2

Sketches in New Orleans by W. A. Rogers 5

New Orleans: French or Spanish?
  A Conversation Overheard in the French Market 7

Lasting Fame of the Explorers of the Mississippi 14

Pere (Jacques) Marquette 15

Brief Outline of Spanish Governors of Louisiana 22

Pedro Rousseau and the Mississippi Squadron 26

Was Jean Lafitte Truly a Pirate? 28

Example of a True Pirate — Sir Henry Morgan 30

Types of Crafts on the Old River Front 36

Easy Money 43

John Law and Paper Money 45

The Old New Orleans Mint 51

New Orleans Becomes Important Port for Importing
  Bananas and Other Tropical Fruit 54

Antique Furniture in Louisiana Before 1860 61

The Medical History of New Orleans 64

The Yellow Fever Period 86

What is a Creole? 90

The German Coast 93

What is the Probable Number of Creoles of German Descent? ...109

The German Language Among the Creoles of Louisiana ...110

A Note on Bienville's Wealth 114

Among Landmarks of New Orleans — The Building
  of the Customhouse 116

History of the Louisiana Sugar Industry 120

ILLUSTRATIONS

Jackson Square 1899	iii
Mardi Gras Carnival Celebration 1899	3
Basket Men — French Market	4
The New Orleans Carnival 1899	6
The French Market	8
New Orleans Defenses 1792 — Showing How the Mississippi Runs	21
Spanish Governors of Louisiana	25
Authentic Picture of Jean Lafitte	27
Keel Boat on the Mississippi	36
Steamboat Edward J. Gay at Dock — New Orleans 1860	40
Canal Street in 1857	46
Picture of the New Orleans Mint	53
Charity Hospital in 1859	66
A Creole Family at the Opera, New Orleans 1871	93
The Customhouse — New Orleans	117
The United States Branch Mint — New Orleans	119
The Louisiana Sugar and Rice Exchange	120
Louisiana Sugar and Molasses Mill	131
A Typical Plantation Home	137

A Brief History of Mardi Gras

Mardi Gras in New Orleans is the "Greatest Free Show on Earth." Hundreds of thousands of citizens and visitors celebrate before the Lenten period of fast. Mardi Gras means Shrove Tuesday (from shrive: 1. to hear confession of — 2. make confession). Mardi Gras in New Orleans covers a period of about two weeks during which the various street parades are held. The Carnival season opens officially on January 6, Twelfth night after Christmas, and is marked by a succession of elaborate private balls.

Origin of Mardi Gras

It is known that several years prior to the founding of New Orleans a party of Frenchmen led by Iberville camped at a place on the Mississippi 30 miles from its mouth on March 3 1699, Mardi Gras day of that year. Iberville named the location "Pointe du Mardi Gras," and it is assumed that some sort of celebration took place, the first of its kind in Louisiana. The party may have done no more than drink wine and bake a catfish, but the occasion was observed. It is said (but there is no definite record) that soon after Bienville founded New Orleans his men held impromptu Mardi Gras celebrations. Such celebrations took the form of balls and masquerade dances, with, perhaps, some street masking, and, no doubt, some drinking. The first newspaper account of an organized street pageant was in 1837.

The street pageants as they are organized today did not begin until 1857. In that year the Mistick Krewe of Comus was organized, and for the first time a parade with torchlights took place. The theme was "The Demon Actors in Milton's Paradise Lost." For more than 150 years the Krewe of Comus has continued to hold its annual ball and parade. But in the meantime many other organizations have been formed.

Rex, King of Carnival, who presides on Mardi Gras Day, made his first appearance in 1872 when Rex Ball was organized. In that same year the Knights of Momus was organized and held a ball and parade on New Year's Eve. The Krewe of Proteus was organized in 1882. Later came such organizations as the Hermes, Carrollton, Okeanos, Orion, Babylon, Adonis, Thoth, Mid-City, Venus, Freret, and Alla.

There are about 65 Carnival organizations in New Orleans. Each gives an annual ball. The average Carnival ball costs about $25,000 to produce. The money required for staging these balls and parades is furnished by members of the Carnival organizations. No tickets are sold. Anybody can see the parade free. Only on invitation can one attend a ball.

The Captains and secret committees select the kings, queens, and courts.

Rex, always an outstanding civic leader, rules as King of Carnival.

Alfred the Great, King of England, celebrated Christmas for 12 days, and January 6 has since been known as Twelfth Day.

MARDI GRAS IN NEW ORLEANS IN 1879
"A Magnificent and Artistic Pageant"

Described in Frank Leslie's Illustrated Newspaper March 22, 1879

Mardi Gras has come and gone, and the Crescent City is in sackcloth and ashes. The mad merry jest has been played out, caps and bells have been laid aside and Tom Fool relegated to the region of oblivion for 363 days, albeit the shadow of a gruesome past hung like a pall over as gallant a cortége as ever rode through town or hamlet in medieval times. The one fatal remembrance asserted itself through the black crepe that mutely appealed to the eye upon every side.

Monday, February 24th (the eve of Mardi Gras), was a bright, warm day, the mercury standing at 60° in the shade. Everybody was in the streets, for His Majesty was announced to arrive by water at 3:30 o'clock, and take possession of the city according to time-honored custom. Canal Street was lined from Rampart to the Levee by a curious, eager, and excited crowd, the dark element being very much in front.

At the time appointed a lily-white tug blowing a whistle much too big for her, came plunging round the bend in the river, followed by a leviathan steamer bearing "Caesar and his Fortunes." Cannon began to boom, bells to ring, thousands of voices to huzza, while every whistle on every steamer exerted itself to the utmost limits of its capacity, becoming hoarse in its anxiety to exhibit a profound and enthusiastic loyalty. In a few minutes, the King's trumpeters appeared on the gangway, followed by the Dukes of the Realm, gorgeous in blue and green and purple velvet, broidered in gold, buff boots to the hips, flowing perukes, and cocked hats richly laced. Then, at a little distance, came His Most Gracious

Majesty, attired in a magnificent costume, copied after the Versailles portrait of Louis Quatorze, "le gran monarque". His reception was such as any potentate might feel fairly proud of, and his gracious affability in bowing responsive to the hearty "viv" that rent the air, bore ample testimony of how deeply the loyal welcome had touched his royal heart.

The Cortége proceeded to the City Hall, on the steps of which the Mayor, bare-headed, received His Majesty, and presented him with the keys of the city, together with a loyal and dutiful address of welcome. From the City Hall the cavalcade moved to the Royal Palace San Carlos (the St. Charles Hotel), and here His Most Gracious Majesty alighted. An undress levee was immediately held, at which many presentations of distinguished personages took place, including several ladies of high degree. In the evening His Majesty, accompanied by several members of the court, attended the theatre. Thus passed the eve of Mardi Gras.

From cockcrow to curfew on Tuesday, the 25th, New Orleans was "en fete". From an early hour Canal Street was a dense mass of expectant humanity, the statue of Henry Clay being a sort of island in the sea of human faces. The day was a perfect glory, a dazzling sunshine, a caressing breeze, a Summer heat.

The Mardi-Gras Carnival Celebration at New Orleans — Maskers of the Street at night. From HARPER'S WEEKLY, Mar. 4, 1899. Drawn by E. L. Blumenschein.

Basket-Men, French Market. Court of Old House, Toulouse and Royal Sts. Old Mansion, French Quarter. In the French Market. Tombs, Old St. Louis Cemetery. Gateway, St. Louis Cemetery. All six illustrations drawn by W. A. Rogers, appearing in HARPER'S WEEKLY, Dec. 30, 1899.

SKETCHES IN NEW ORLEANS
By W. A. Rogers
(from *Harper's Weekly*, December 30, 1899, p. 1327; see illustrations)

"New Orleans is one of the places where a Northern man's preconceived ideas of things are of no use to him. Women do their Christmas shopping in sun-bonnets; carpenters are employed to build cisterns, and build them up in the air; and the dead are buried from one to twenty feet above the ground. Roses bloom in January; drivers of heavy trucks pull up short to allow pedestrians to pass; and the wise man puts on his overcoat when he gets into the house.

"Traffic on the public highways in the neighborhood of the Court House is suspended while the honorable court is in session, a court attendant putting up a heavy chain barrier across St. Ann's Street, St. Peter's Street, and Chartres Street when court opens in the morning.

"In the old portion of New Orleans, the French quarter, the rich and the poor live closer together than in any other American city I could name. Many old mansions, fine examples of classical and Colonial architecture, are going to decay, the one feature remaining in its original beauty being the grill-work railings and brackets that adorn the balconies and porches. These old homes are at present occupied for the most part by the very poor; yet, opening from the most unpromising streets, an occasional arched passageway leads into a court set out in fine formal old fashion. The court shown in the picture is a fair type of many of them, but there are more elaborate ones, with palms, banana-trees, roses, chrysanthemums, and many flowering shrubs, and walks of white shells. Here, in a house almost surrounding the court, dwell some old families of creoles, who cling to the quaint neighborhood even in its decadence. On some of the buildings are emblematic figures in stucco-work and in wood-carving — the pelican (the emblem of the State) appearing on many of the old buildings, notably the State arsenal near Jackson Square.

"New Orleans is just now in the throes of a great change from the old ways. The streets are torn up all over the city for electrical subways, and sewers and a new water supply. The old pavements, formed of stone blocks about the size of a travelling-bag, are to give way to asphalt. When these improvements are accomplished the town will be as delightful to live in as it has always been to visit, always provided that the old French quarter is never modernized out of existence. There are some features of the French market that it is to be hoped may always be in evidence — the great round baskets, for instance, which the market-men carry about on their heads, and the wonderful sun-bonnets the women wear. The Northern sun-bonnet is a tame affair beside these gorgeous creations that bloom on Southern streets."

In 1899 New Orleans Carnival came on February 14, 'amid snow and ice. Snow fell to a depth of three inches. The temperature got down to as low as 7 degrees. (From HARPER'S WEEKLY, March 4, 1899.)

NEW ORLEANS: FRENCH OR SPANISH?

A Conversation Overheard in the French Market

After attending a Carnival ball I was sitting at a table in the French Market in New Orleans drinking a cup of the delicious coffee which is served there, eating doughnuts (which are called beignets), of a kind that cannot be found anywhere else. The place was crowded, for to visit the French Market for coffee and doughnuts after the Carnival balls is a time-honored custom. Next to my table sat two gentlemen in full dress who had come from the same ball which I had attended.

As one slowly sipped his coffee he said to the other, "Henri, the food and service here and the very atmosphere are French. But this is not a French market; it was built by the Spanish in 1791."

Henri put down his cup of coffee and stared at his companion as if he had been challenged. "Alfonso," he said, "do not say that. This was a French city. You should know that. Everything was French: the streets, Bourbon, Chartres, Dauphine, Burgundy, St. Louis, and hundreds of others. There are a few streets with Spanish names, I admit: Carondelet, Galvez, Miro, Salcedo. Maybe twenty-five, maybe more. But French names predominate."

Alfonso, his countenance thoughtful, put a lump of sugar in his coffee and took a bite of his doughnut. "You should know, Henri," he said, "that New Orleans is essentially a city of Spanish creation."

"Don't say that," insisted Henri. "I tell you the customs were and are today French; so is the food, the cooking and the language. How many persons here can speak Spanish? Do you know? No, you don't. But you can find thousands speaking French — some don't know any other language."

In an attempt to make room for a party of pretty young girls, and their escorts, all in evening dress, the waiters moved my table closer to the two gentlemen in whose conversation I was interested. This pleased me.

"I will tell you this," said Alfonso, "the French made a complete failure of colonization. The city didn't begin to grow until the Spanish took it over. And as to the buildings, you must remember that the fire of 1788 destroyed nearly every house or edifice built by the French. And the fire of 1794 swept away more than two hundred dwellings. It would be hard to find a building in the city erected during the French regime, with the exception of the Ursuline Convent on Char-

THE FAMOUS FRENCH MARKET
Located in the heart of the French Quarter, near the great Mississippi River and but a stones throw from celebrated Jackson Square, this venerated place of sales has served the people of New Orleans more than a century.

tres Street, and perhaps a few old buildings which the two great fires didn't destroy or which have withstood the ravages of time."

Henri reached in his pocket for a pack of Picayune cigarettes, and offered one to Alfonso. "This is a Picayune, originated in New Orleans by French people. Have one; they are satisfying."

Alfonso refused. "Cigarettes are bad for you, whether French or Spanish." He took a cigar from his pocket. "I smoke Cuban cigars."

"I really can't argue without a Picayune," said Henri. "You know, at this moment I am thinking of writing a book to show how difficult it was for the different nationalities, the French, the Spanish, and the Americans to amalgamate, to become one and the same people banded together for the government and defense of one great nation. They were in the beginning jealous of one another, envious of one another's achievements in politics and industry. But today we discuss the matter calmly and without prejudice."

"I don't admit that," said Alfonso. "You are highly prejudiced. You can only see the French in the whole picture. That was the fault of the French colonists, they could only see France, the magnificent, the cultured, the powerful, when she was in fact a corrupt, bankrupt nation that considered them only as a great burden. They didn't build and organize in the true sense, for they did not consider themselves Louisianians but Frenchmen camping out, hoping some day when they had made their fortune to return to the mother country. Pardon me if I have put it bluntly, Henri."

"That you have done," said Henri in disgust. "Indeed such a thing never occurred to me. As a matter of fact it never occurred to anybody but you, Alfonso."

These men both spoke English with a cultivated Creole accent, and I could not be certain that they were French and Spanish; only their prejudices and their names indicated that they were.

Alfonso pulled heavily on his cigar and blew puffs of smoke into the air. "Please forgive me, Henri," he said. "I see you are sensitive on this matter. I will admit that the French inhabitants labored under great difficulties, and considering their scant opportunities did well enough to be acclaimed the founders of the great city of New Orleans and the colony which became the state of Louisiana."

"Well," said Henri, "I'm glad you admit that. As a matter of fact you agree with me; facts are, of course, convincing."

"No, I don't," said Alfonso. "You interrupted me. I was going to say this: but the magnificent French court was lax in the support of the colony. The conservative Spanish government under Charles III, after the transfer of the territory to Spain, was lavish in its contributions to the colony's success. I'm sure you know that although the transfer was made secretly in 1761 Spain did not take over until 1764. Read the Spanish Regime in Missouri by Louis Houck. That is a fine history of Louisiana."

"I have read everything on the subject," said Henri. "I can tell you all about Jean Milhet's visit to France in an effort to persuade the King to let Louisiana remain a French province. He failed. I know the names of the prominent citizens of Louisiana who supported Jean Milhet in the plan, and who were later considered conspirators and were shot in the Place d'Armes by O'Reilly. I know about Ulloa's foolhardiness which caused him to be expelled from the colony. I know that Unzaga and Galvez were the first real gentlemen the Spanish government sent here. I can tell you of the valiant Captain Pierre George Rousseau who, though a Frenchman, was one of the most trusted men in the Spanish service. All the Spanish governors of Louisiana from Galvez to the Louisiana Purchase often relied upon him rather than upon their own men to conduct important missions. I repeat he was a Frenchman."

"Yes," said Alfonso, "I know about him. He was first an officer in the Continental navy."

"That is true," said Henri, "but he was a Frenchman."

"So was Charles Aubry a Frenchman," observed Alfonso. "He betrayed his own people. He gave O'Reilly the names of the men who objected to Spanish rule. They were the colony's most eminent men, and his friends. But he called them conspirators to please O'Reilly. There was no greater rascal in the colony."

"For that matter," said Henri, "you are likely to find traitors anywhere. You can't judge a population by one man, can you?"

"We are digressing," said Alfonso. "Our question is whether New Orleans was built by the French or the Spanish. Although I hardly think it is debatable."

"Don't say that, Alfonso, for I know you mean that I'm disputing evident facts," said Henri.

Alfonso was thoughtful as he drained his cup and then puffed vigorously at his cigar. "You know, Henri, I'm thinking that a Spaniard, DeSoto, discovered the Mississippi River; a Frenchman, LaSalle, explored it; and a Frenchman, Pere Marquette, found that it flowed into the Gulf of Mexico. Even after the Louisiana Purchase the Americans explored. No river in the Western Hemisphere has been so thoroughly and completely explored."

"You forgot to say," reminded Henri, "that Pierre George Rousseau explored, too, and made an excellent map of the river. He was also a member of the Pike expedition, and probably was of much value, for in addition to his acquaintance with the river he could speak the four languages used in the territory."

"Yes, that's true," recalled Alfonso: "I read something about him somewhere. I think Gayoso and Carondelet mentioned him frequently. But why do you push him forward? Because he was a Frenchman?"

"No," said Henri, "because he was a man of many accomplishments who received scant mention in the histories of Louisiana."

"I wouldn't say that," suggested Alfonso. "I've frequently run across him in my reading."

"Then," said Henri, "you have read Houck's Spanish Regime in Missouri and his History of Missouri. There you will find an account of his career as a soldier in Louisiana."

"Yes," said Alfonso, "I have read it. But I have also read in Herbert Asbury's book, THE FRENCH QUARTER, that Grace King said after the fires of 1788 and 1794 what lay in the ashes was, at best, but an irregular, ill-built French town, while what arose from them was a stately Spanish city, proportioned with grace and built with solidity. There is also a saying that the Spaniards found the city a town of hovels and left it a city of palaces."

Henri hesitated for a moment, while he lit another Picayune cigarette. Finally he answered: "You don't expect me to believe that, Alfonso, because Grace King said it. It is a phrase, well arranged, I admit, but not entirely a fact. There were some fine buildings destroyed in those fires."

At this moment a friend of these two gentlemen approached their table.

"Oh, there's Robert," exclaimed Henri. "Come and have coffee with us. Pull up a chair."

There was a vacant chair at my table, and I offered it to the gentleman. Alfonso stood up and placed the chair at the table for his friend, thanking me politely.

"We are in a heated argument, Robert," said Henri. "Alfonso says that New Orleans is a city of Spanish creation. I say it is of French. I say many of the customs are still French, and many of the people are French. What do you say?"

"Well," said Robert, "I call it an American city. It didn't really amount to much until the Americans took it over — then it grew by leaps and bounds."

"Oh," said Henri, "you don't know what we're talking about. I say in the beginning the French built it. Alfonso says the Spanish made it a real city."

Alfonso lifted up three fingers as a waiter passed his table and promptly coffee and doughnuts were served.

"You're out late, Robert, if you haven't been to a ball," said Henri.

"Yes, I am," admitted Robert. "I've been working at the office. We're having a stockholders' meeting tomorrow, and I had to complete the report of what we did and didn't do."

"I know all about that," said Alfonso. "But since you are widely read we are very anxious to have your opinion on the subject under discussion. I mean your thoughtful, serious opinion."

"Well," said Robert, "it's a matter I've thought little about. But if I recall correctly, Louisiana was a poor colony until the Spanish came. From the standpoint of an economist, which I am by profession, as you know, a city's prosperity is judged by its trade, imports and exports. The exports of the entire colony the year before the Spanish domination were only about two hundred and fifty thousand dollars. The population of the entire colony was, I think, only thirteen thousand; New Orleans proper was, I believe, three thousand or around that figure. The exports indicate there was little prosperity."

This statement did not please Henri. "Do you really think that is important?" he asked. "Are you not aware that the French were a very cultured people? Read the letters and newspapers of that period and you will realize that what you call the poor French settlers were well educated, and their social life was after the fashion of the people of Paris or London. If you had attended one of their parties in an unpainted shack, equipped with home-made furniture, you would have been compelled to observe the rules of etiquette in the strictest sense."

"Indeed I had not thought of that," said Robert. "But since you and Alfonso are taking opposite sides — I wonder why."

"That is because his ancestors were mostly French," said Alfonso, "and mine were Spanish."

Robert was amused. "I think I know you both very well, and I would say that you are Americans, just as I am. Tell me, Alfonso, do you speak Spanish?"

"No, Robert, I don't — only a few words but everybody knows that much."

"Was your mother Spanish?"

"Yes," said Alfonso, "she was Spanish."

"And your grandfather on her side?"

"He had a Spanish name but he was Spanish and English."

"And your grandmother — but you told me, she was English."

"Yes, that is right."

"And they were born in this country?"

"Yes."

"Then you are an American."

Robert then faced Henri. "Was your father a Frenchman?"

"I can say, yes, he was," replied Henri; "my people were a mixture of French, Spanish, English, and Irish. They were all here before the Revolution."

"Do you speak French, Henri?"

"I understand it."

"But you don't speak the language."

"No, I can't say that I do."

"Then," said Robert, "there is no justifiable prejudice in this argument; it is purely an academic discussion. Let's go home; it's late."

They went home. And I had another cup of coffee.

I felt certain that Henri (whoever he was) had no serious intention of writing a book as he threatened to do during the discussion. But I felt an urge at that moment to go out and search archives and to gather information wherever I could. This urge did not leave me. The romance and tragedy in the history of the old territory which was called Louisiana and the great river, the Mississippi, became more and more interesting as I searched and found documents, many of which had never been published.

Lasting Fame of the Explorers of the Mississippi

The Mississippi River, 2,350 miles in length, is the longest river in North America; that alone gives it importance, but it is also the great drainage system for Mid-America. It is the gateway to the Gulf of Mexico from which vessels sail to all ports of the world, and its tributaries, the Ohio, the Missouri, the Arkansas, and the Red River are also great streams. It is truly what the Indians called it (and which the name means) **the Father of Waters.** Its history is fraught with adventure, romance and tragedy perhaps excelling that of any other river in the Western Hemisphere. The names of its discoverers and explorers are immortal, and there would be great interest in any spot, if found, where they pitched their tents for a night. Towns sprang up along its banks and became great cities but little did the discoverers and explorers of this great stream know what fame they had achieved.

The source of the Mississippi is a small lake in upper Minnesota, one hundred and seventy miles from the Canadian border. Here a small stream meanders slowly southward. The absence of difficult waterfalls has made the Mississippi an easy river to travel by boat and yet three centuries passed between the time when white men first saw the river and the time of the discovery of the source in Minnesota. Some of the reasons for this lag are geographical but the more important reasons concern the explorers and the nations they represented. The river was controlled during various periods by the Spanish, French, British and Americans and each nation was concerned with protecting its sovereignty more than with exploring the river to find its source.

If DeSoto could arise from his grave under the current of the great river, he would be astonished to see counties, hotels, buildings, automobiles, schools, ships, and villages named after him. He would wonder why, for he was mainly searching for treasure while exploring the country. Hernando DeSoto, Knight of Santiago, Hidalgo of Badajoz, is and was an enigma. He was one of the most successful men of his time and yet was also one of the biggest failures. He has been accepted as the first white man to have seen the Mississippi but when he saw the river he did not appreciate the importance of his discovery.

The year Columbus discovered the New World was also the year when Granada surrendered and brought to an end nearly eight centuries of fighting in an attempt to drive the Moors from the Iberian peninsula. The end of fighting left an experienced body of professional soldiers with little employment. These were the conquistadors and the story of Hernando DeSoto is tightly interwoven with their achievements. As a subaltern DeSoto saw action in Panama; as a senior lieutenant he made a fortune in Peru; and as a general he was defeated in North America.

Marquette, Joliet, and LaSalle would be equally astonished, were they to arise with DeSoto, to see their names immortal throughout the land, and their fame known to every schoolboy.

The trail was blazed, it is true, but the men who came in the wake of the discoverers and explorers to clear the land and render it safe from aggressors were not less worthily engaged. But for their energy and skill the country would still be a wilderness, and the fame of the discoverers and explorers would have been buried with them.

LaSalle himself, entering the Mississippi from the Illinois River on February 6, 1682, actually traveled to the Gulf of Mexico, and having done so, erected a cross on the shore and took possession of the country, including the river and the entire Mississippi Valley, in the name of Louis XIV. He named it Louisiana. DeSoto had already taken possession in the name of the King of Spain (Charles I on whose empire "the sun never set") but that was 143 years before; the incident and the wilderness had been forgotten. LaSalle went to France and persuaded Louis XIV to permit him to establish a colony on the Mississippi River. Having obtained permission, he started out with four ships and high hopes. But he could not find the mouth of the river; he missed it on his way and landed in what is now Texas. As a matter of fact, he could not find the Mississippi at all but found a stream in Texas known as the Lavaca River, and established a fort where he left the greater number of his men (to perish) while he went on with a small party and searched for the Mississippi. He never found it. The men who followed him grew weary and impatient. They realized that they were following a leader who did not know where he was going and were suffering hardships almost unbearable. Stubborn, unreasonable, imperious, he would take no advice. He had previously discovered the Ohio and the Illinois rivers, and explored the Mississippi. It was ridiculous that, having been so eminently successful, he should now acknowledge that he was lost and incapable of finding his way. But his men were tired-to-the-bones. When they could endure no further they assassinated him and went their way.

PERE (JACQUES) MARQUETTE

It was unfortunate for LaSalle that he did not have Pere

Marquette's map of the Mississippi, as crude as it was, made from memory (for the original had been lost when his boat sank) but still indicating accurately the course of the river. It had been resting unnoticed in the archives of Paris since 1675.

Pere Marquette as an individual is the most interesting of all the explorers of the Mississippi. He carried on his work so modestly and in so unspectacular a manner that his deeds, as great as they were, are scarcely remembered, except by students of history. He was a saintly man and rendered a great service to his country without destroying others, which is an uncommon achievement among the heroes of history.

Father James Marquette began his life in the ancient village of Laon on the River Oise in 1637. The Marquettes were of the very oldest families of this village, and, like other families of that place, they led an easy life, except in times of war, for they were all in some manner attached to the military profession. None of them, except James, gave much luster to the name.

At the age of 17 young Marquette, already tired of a secular life, decided that he wanted to become a Jesuit, and to that end he worked and prayed unceasingly. He had been instructed by his pious mother, Rosa de la Salle, whose relative, John Baptiste de la Salle, founded the Brothers of the Christian School, and with her influence to support him in his ambition he soon attained his goal — he became a Jesuit. But this was only the first step towards his real ambition — to become a traveling missionary.

His devotion to his work and his outstanding ability attracted attention. Everybody in Laon looked up to him, for the nobility of his heart brought him affection and respect. Children loved him for something that was fine in his soul, they knew not what it was. Unlike the clergy of his times, he was not severe, but lovable and understanding. He was, after all, teaching the doctrines of Christ. Why should he not follow His example as nearly as he could? He never tried to make an impression; he did not like to be talked about. He simply loved his fellowman, and believed that in every human soul there was something noble. If he did not discover even in the wayward a redeeming quality, he endowed the person with one. Faith in humanity was necessary to him. He could not work without it.

When as a young priest he went out upon the streets of Laon he merely engaged his friends in pleasant conversation, but did not preach to them, for he knew that they had available to them all the information that he had gathered. He wanted to go to people who had never heard of Christ. He felt that it was his mission in life to teach them. Every day he knelt in front of the altar of his church and prayed that he might be given the opportunity to go among people who had not been given the advantage of the message that Christ brought to the City of Jerusalem, expecting that it would be heard all over the earth. His health was not particularly good; he was not naturally strong. But he did not consider this in making his decision. He ignored his spells of illness; he never called a doctor, but recovered in due time. The body naturally mends itself. Prayer often helps.

At long last his prayers were answered. He was appointed a traveling missionary. This, he knew, was a life fraught with hardships and disappointments. In the summer of 1666 he was sent to Canada. The voyage was long and tiresome, but when he arrived and saw the great forest in bloom he was happy, and knelt down upon the ground and thanked God that he had been able to witness so wonderful a scene. He was not in the least bewildered by his new surroundings and the task he had to perform. He went immediately among the Indians who traded at Tadoussac, and began to teach them. He had not mastered their language, but told them in his own way why he had come. They were struck by his manner and appearance: he was of medium size, with stooping shoulders, but his countenance invited trust. They paid him respect in their way.

He remained at Tadoussac for nearly two years, and while there he mastered the language of the Indian tribes with which he had to deal. They were slow to learn French. He could be more convincing teaching them in their own language. It was easy to contact them during trading season, but when they scattered and went into winter quarters they were hard to reach. This did not deter Pere Marquette: he carried the gospel among them wherever they were, and whenever he appeared he was welcome, for they knew that he had waded through the snow to find them. Huddled near the fires in their wigwams they would say in substance: "You come as our friend; you tell us the Great Teacher says do not kill, do not steal, do not fight, and the Great Christ will take care of us." He told them that Christ taught mankind how to live, not how to die, and if they lived as He taught them to, they would never die, but would go on living through eternity. The greater number of the tribes heeded carefully what he had to say. Some preferred their own way of life.

Pere Marquette did not notice any of the hardships which he encountered. He was leading what he considered a pleasant life. He found pleasure in the beautiful snow and the leafless trees in winter, the green foliage in the spring and summer, and the varied colors of the shedding trees of autumn. He found pleasure, too, in human beings, their emotions, their faith in him and what he taught. Most men in his condition would have felt very sorry for themselves, and would have recorded in great detail the privations they suffered. Pere Marquette wrote only of the pleasure he derived from his work and the beauty that surrounded him. There is a difference between a famous man and a great man. Many famous men are often egotistical and petty. Pere Marquette was a great man!

He never tired of a place and the friends he made, but when he felt that he had virtually "converted" a tribe of Indians it was his duty to move on to a new field. He left reluctantly, for it was his nature to love people and places. He always moved westward, for there was a charm about the newly discovered country of the interior where few white men had ever set foot. In 1668 he established the mission at Sault Sainte Marie. There he remained for about two years, and then went on to Mackinaw where he built the first chapel. It was entirely a log structure. From here he went to La Pointe, near Lake Superior, where there was a large Indian settlement, and near where now stands the City of Ashland, in the State of Wisconsin.

At La Pointe Pere Marquette found a depraved group of Indians. They were for the most part refugees who had escaped from the Iroquois War which started in 1642. They were a diseased and disheartened people, who did not believe in their own Great Spirit, and were, of course, unwilling to accept Christ. They had been bred in treachery. To convert them to Christianity was to be Marquette's hardest task. He knew that, but he was not discouraged. They deceived him, they lied, and they laughed at his doctrines, but they respected him. He did not lose faith in them nor in himself. The thing that impressed these depraved Indians more than all was the fact that Indians (whom he had taught before) living "30 days' journey from La Pointe" came to question him concerning Christianity and the church, and to invite him to visit them. No other missionary had been so honored.

The French in those times had hope that a way to China could be found through the western rivers and lakes. Maybe the Mississippi would take them to China. They did not know. Nobody had so far followed the Mississippi to its mouth. The Spaniards had abandoned it for the time being and gone to Mexico and West Florida. Pere Marquette was interested in this question. He had not abandoned his purpose to teach the Indians Christianity, but he could not resist the lure of adventure and the opportunity to explore the new country. He had met Louis Joliet while he was stationed at Sault Sainte Marie, and they had become friends. Joliet had admired Marquette's keen intelligence, and when he was appointed to the enterprise of discovering the outlet of the Mississippi he asked Marquette to accompany him.

There had been many opinions concerning where the "Messi-sippi" flowed. Father Allouz had heard from the Indians who lived on the great river called the "Messipi" that the river flowed into the seas of Virginia. The Indians, strangely enough, did not seem to know where the Mississippi flowed. There were those among the Indians and the white men who thought that it flowed into the Gulf of California or the Gulf of Mexico. Nobody was sure. It was left to Louis Joliet and Pere Marquette to settle the question.

They set out from Mackinaw, and, making their way in birch-bark canoes to the head of Green Bay, they traveled up the Fox River to Portage; here they carried their canoes a short distance overland to the Wisconsin River, whose current bore them into the broad and swift-flowing Mississippi, which the Indians called the Father of Waters. They turned southward, and decided to let the current bear them where it would. They drifted onward and passed the mouth of the Missouri. In a few weeks they came to the spot where De Soto had crossed the Mississippi more than a hundred years before. That was about at the northwest corner of the State of Mississippi. This impressed Marquette, for he was ever ready to overlook and forgive, but probably Joliet recalled that De Soto was more a cruel plunderer than he was an explorer, for he wanted to push on rather than remain to pay special reverence to the historic spot.

They reached the mouth of the Arkansas River, and there some Indians told them that the tribes below were hostile to white men, and they had better not risk the journey. They were not far from what is now the northern boundary of Louisiana. They had, in fact, accomplished their purpose. They knew that the Mississippi flowed into the Gulf of Mexico. The Indians they met, who were in a position to know, told them so. They turned back.

Paddling upstream under the burning sun was a hard task. It was, in fact, too much for Marquette, whose strength was already waning. He did not complain.

When they reached the Illinois they decided to change their route homeward, and went up that river to an Indian village just below Ottawa. From there they made their way across Lake Michigan.

Marquette, who was an able writer, made a careful record of all they saw and the pleasures they found on the journey. But their canoe was wrecked in the rapids above Montreal, and his papers so carefully written were lost. He afterwards wrote an account of the journey from memory. Joliet helped him recall what had happened. But Joliet did not see what Marquette saw. Marquette saw the hills, the sandy bottoms, the woods, green and amber, and a glorious red and brown, the fertile land that produced abundant vegetation, the prairies. "Here," he writes, "you find oaks, walnuts, whitewoods, and other kinds of trees with branches armed with thorns." He called the river "La Conception." The name did not last. The Spaniards called it "Espiritu Santo." LaSalle christened it "Colbert." None of these names endured. The Indian name, Mississippi, the Great River, was in the end accepted.

Pere Marquette had great dreams on this journey. But such a vast and beautiful country would make a savage dream, much less a man of Marquette's imagination and intelligence. He saw the opportunity to build a great French empire and to bring to it the teachings of Christ. But Louis XIV did not have Pere Marquette's capacity and vision; without his support no empire could be built. "I do not despair," he wrote, "of some day being able to publish the gospel to all nations of the New World who have long been plunged in darkness."

He had now mastered the tongues of six Indian tribes, and could in a manner communicate with all the tribes of North America. He was at home with them all; they were his people and North America was his home. He knew the country so well that when he made a map of it and lost it in the rapids he was able to reproduce it from memory. This map was sent to France in 1674 and his reports were sent to the Mission of Sault Sainte Marie, but in 1675 the French Government took possession of them and placed them in the archives at Paris. They were published, however, in 1681, and were of great interest to the men who continued to explore the Mississippi Valley.

Pere Marquette tells the story of the journey from the full heart of a missionary. He had a pleasant journey; all his journeys were, in fact, pleasant, as his life was, for the whole world which God created was to him a thing of beauty; and in his heart there was always a hope for the future. If he lived in a dream it was a great dream, worthy of the finest intellect. At least he foresaw that something of great moment would spring up in the land that he loved; if not a French empire, something great. It was to be, though he did not know, the United States of America.

Pere Marquette, forever seeing a rainbow in the sky, for that was a pleasant thing to see, did not notice that he was succumbing to toil and exposure when he reached middle life. Even on the way back from his journey with Joliet he became very ill. This was at Green Bay in 1674. He was then only 37. After a while his strength returned, and he went on with his work, ignoring the advice of his friends, that he should slow down and rest in bed; even the Indians cautioned him, telling him that it was not wise to travel far. But he would not stop.

He went on in spite of all warnings, but had gone no farther than the site of Chicago when his strength failed again, and there he spent the winter, holding on to life by sheer will, for he felt that his work was not done. He suffered, but made no complaint; he prayed, and spoke cheerfully. The Indians frequently visited him, for they loved him with all their capacity. At last, again somewhat stronger in 1675, he went to Kaskaskia, and ministered there for a time, going from wigwam to wigwam, and feeling great joy in spreading the truth of Christianity. No other man in missionary work had won so many converts.

His health failed again, and he was taken a short distance northward by the Indians to die. They treated him well. But daily he grew weaker. On the way up Lake Michigan he told them of the great joy that awaited him. In sorrow they bore him to a beautiful spot on the shore of the lake, and there he asked to be left alone for a time, for he needed to pray and sleep. He said that he would know when death was coming and would call them. So he did. His death, like his life, was pleasant. He saw glories awaiting him.

He was buried where he died. But a year later some Ottawa Indians carried his bones to the mission of St. Ignace at Mackinaw, and buried them under his chapel of logs. In 1877, when an excavation of the place was made, for the chapel had burned, some bones were found, and priests of that section, believing them to be the bones of Marquette, reburied them. But what are bones! The spirit of Marquette lives in Wisconsin: his name will be there forever. In appreciation, the State of Wisconsin has placed a monument to him in Washington, D. C.

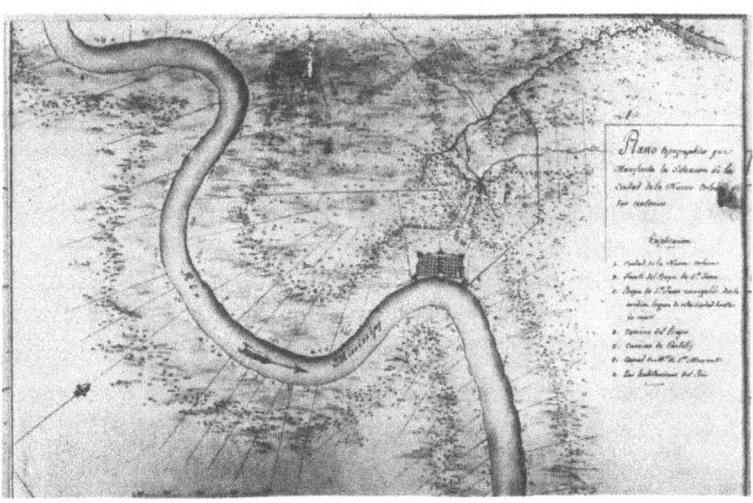

NEW ORLEANS DEFENSES — 1792. Showing how the Mississippi runs.

BRIEF OUTLINE OF SPANISH GOVERNORS OF LOUISIANA

1. **Antonio de Ulloa y de la Torre Guiral**
   a. Appointed April 30, May 21, 1765.
   b. Arrives at New Orleans on **El Volante,** March 5, 1766.
   c. Raises flag over Louisiana, but not at New Orleans, January 20, 1767.
   d. Protest demonstrations force him to flee for safety, October 28, 1768.
   e. Superior Council banishes Ulloa, October 29, 1768.
   f. Ulloa leaves on French ship from Balize to Havana, November 16, 1768.

2. **Alexander O'Reilly y McDowell**
   a. Appointed to establish Spanish law and power, April 16, 1769.
   b. Leads expedition from Havana to New Orleans, July 6, 1769.
   c. Takes formal possession of New Orleans in impressive ceremonies, August 18, 1769.
   d. Arrests leaders of 1768 revolt, August 21, 1769.
   e. Executes six leaders and imprisons six others, October 25, 1769.
   f. Issues proclamations and ordinances for governing Louisiana, August 24, 1769 - February 23, 1770.
   g. O'Reilly leaves Louisiana for Havana, March 1, 1770.

3. **Luis Unzaga y Amezaga**
   a. O'Reilly administers oath of office to him, December 1, 1769.
   b. Unzaga presides over first New Orleans Cabildo, December 2, 1769.
   c. When O'Reilly leaves for Cuba, Unzaga is sole governor, March 1, 1770.
   d. Spain confirms Unzaga as governor, August 17, 1772.
   e. Unzaga swears in his successor, Gálvez, January 1, 1777.
   f. Miró conducts **residencia** (judicial inquiry) on Unzaga's term as governor, 1786-1787.

4. **Bernardo de Galvez Madrid Cabrera Ramirez y Marquez**
   a. Appointed governor, September 19, 1776.
   b. Sworn in at New Orleans by Unzaga, January 1, 1777.
   c. Crown appoints Gálvez governor in proprietorship, May 8, 1779.

- d. Cabildo of New Orleans swears him in as governor, August 20, 1779.
- e. Gálvez places Pedro Piernas as acting governor while he leads expedition against British West Florida posts, August 27, 1779.
- f. Gálvez named captain-general of Louisiana and West Florida as they are separated from the Cuban government, February 12, 1781.
- g. Gálvez turns government over to Esteban Miró on ad-interim basis and leaves for Caribbean campaign, 1782.
- h. Gálvez given double appointment as captain-general of Cuba as well as captain-general of Louisiana and the two Floridas.
- i. Gálvez becomes viceroy of New Spain (Mexico) but retains also the post of captain-general of Louisiana and the Floridas (1785).
- j. Gálvez dies and Joseph de Ezpeleta becomes both captain-general of Cuba and captain-general of Louisiana and the Floridas, November 30, 1786.
- k. Royal decree exempts Gálvez from **residencia,** May 7, 1788.

5. **Esteban Rodriguez Miro y Sabater**
   - a. Named colonel commanding the Louisiana Infantry Regiment, February 15, 1781.
   - b. Named governor ad-interim by Gálvez and left in charge of Louisiana, 1782.
   - c. Appointed governor in proprietorship, July 14, 24, 1785.
   - d. Swears in his successor, the Baron de Carondelet, December 30, 1791.
   - e. Crown at first exempts Miró from **residencia,** later changes mind.
   - f. Judge Jaen takes **residencia** of Miró and finds him guiltless of charges, 1803-1804.

6. **Luis Francisco Hector, Baron de Carondelet de Noyelles, Seigneur d'Haine Saint Pierre**
   - a. Appointed governor-general of Louisiana while still governor of El Salvador in Central America, March 17, 1791.
   - b. Sworn in by Miró in New Orleans, December 30, 1791.
   - c. When captain-generals of Havana change, Carondelet becomes commander-general of Louisiana ad-interim, with right to correspond directly with Spain, May 24, 1796.

d. Appointed president of the Audiencia of Quito in Ecuador, October 28, 1796.
   e. Swears in successor, Gayoso, August 5, 1797.
   f. Gayoso conducts secret **residencia** of Carondelet, August 7, 1797.

7. **Manuel Luis Gayoso de Lemos y Amorin**
   a. Appointed governor of Natchez District in West Florida, November 3, 1787.
   b. Sworn in as governor of Natchez District, May 25, 1789.
   c. Appointed governor-general of Louisiana, October 28, 1796.
   d. Sworn in by Carondelet at New Orleans, August 5, 1797.
   e. Dies of yellow fever and is buried in Cathedral, July 18, 1799.

8. **Interim-governors of Louisiana**
   a. Lieutenant-governor, Dr. Nicholás María Vidal, takes political and religious command, July 19, 1799.
   b. Commander of Louisiana Infantry Regiment, Col. Francisco Bouligny, takes military command of province, July 19, 1799.

9. **Sebastian Calvo de la Puerta y O'Farrell, Marques de Casa-Calvo**
   a. Appointed ad-interim governor-general of Louisiana in charge of military by captain-general Marqué de Someruelos of Cuba, September 18, 1799.
   b. Appointed commissioner to deliver Louisiana to France, January 18, 1803.
   c. Returns to Louisiana with orders to deliver Louisiana, April 10, 1803.
   d. Casa-Calvo and Salcedo deliver Louisiana to French prèfect Laussat, November 30, 1803.
   e. As boundary commissioner, conducts inspection of physical and historical evidence for western Louisiana boundary, October 1805 - February 4, 1806.

10. **Manuel Juan de Salcedo**
    a. Appointed last governor-general of Louisiana, November 18, 1799.
    b. Officially takes over as military governor-general with pay retroactive to previous day, July 15, 1801.
    c. Issues proclamation that Spain will surrender Louisiana to France, May 18, 1803.
    d. With Casa-Calvo he delivers Louisiana to France, November 30, 1803.

Bernardo de Galvez (1746-1786) Copy of original in National Museum (Mexico), in Fortier's History of Louisiana.

Francisco Luis Hector Baron de Carondelet (1747-1807) From contemporary painting belonging to Duque de Bailen (Madrid). Copy in Fortier's History of Louisiana.

Estevan Miro (1744-1795) From contemporary portrait owned by Baron Edouard Pontalba, Senlis, France. In Fortier's History of Louisiana.

Governor Manuel Gayoso de Lemos (1747-1799) in Brigadier's uniform. From Jack D. L. Holmes "Gallagos Notables en La Luisiana," Cuadernos de Estudios Gallegos, LVII (1964). Facing 104.

Pedro Rousseau and the Mississippi Squadron

When Spain dominated the lower Mississippi Valley after the American Revolution, one of the best means of defense was the unusual Mississippi Squadron. Originally suggested to Governor-general Carondelet by Natchez Governor Manuel Gayoso de Lemos, the fleet consisted of various galleys, galiots, gunboats and cannon launches. The commanders of the various craft were, oddly enough, all career army men, not naval officers at all! From its creation in 1792 until 1796, the commandant of all naval forces on the Mississippi was Pedro Rousseau.

Rousseau was born in France in 1751 and had served as a naval officer in the Virginia and Continental naval forces during the early years of the American Revolution. As captain of militia, he served as second-in-command under Captain William Pickles, an American soldier-of-fortune who fought against the British posts and settlements near New Orleans. As commander of the brig "Galveztown," Rousseau carried General Bernardo de Gálvez past the English cannon at Pensacola in 1781 and gave Spain a victory which swept the British banners from Florida.

Shortly after his appointment in 1792 as commandant of the Mississippi Squadron, Captain Rousseau commanded the troops in an expedition led by José de Evia to capture the remarkable adventurer, William Augustus Bowles, who had taken a trading post at St. Marks, Florida. Rousseau cruised the Mississippi during 1793 and, with Gayoso at his side in 1795, he helped to found the vital post of San Fernando de las Barrancas, present-day Memphis.

The Rousseau tradition for military service was passed on to Pedro's descendants. His oldest son, Pedro Andrés, served in the Louisiana Infantry Regiment, a Spanish unit stationed at New Orleans. Another son, Gustave Sebastian, graduated from West Point in 1828 and achieved distinction during the Mexican War. Lawrence, who was born in New Orleans in 1790, commanded the U.S. Brazil Squadron before the Civil War and helped to build or requisition the first ships for the Confederacy in 1861. The Rousseau name lives on in the person of Lieutenant Thomas Harrison Rousseau, a graduate of West Point who served in Viet Nam, and a descendant of Theodore Rousseau, who settled in Jamestown, Virginia, in 1701, and was the grandfather of the prominent Union general Lovell Harrison Rousseau during the Civil War.

Lieutenant Thomas Harrison Rousseau III is a graduate of the United States Military Academy, West Point (Class of June 1961). His father, Lt. Colonel Thomas Harrison Rousseau, Jr., was decorated twice in World War II, and died while in the service of his country, in Germany. His maternal grandmother, Mrs. Mary C. Easterling, who has been a member of the Mississippi State Bar since 1915, served on the staff of Legal Section, SCAP (Supreme Commander of the Allied Powers) and on the staff of the Judge Advocate, Far East Command, Tokyo, the only lady to serve as an attorney on General McArthur's staff. Upon the signing of the Administrative Agreement between Japan and the United States in 1952, she served with the Judge Advocate, Far East Air Force, a total of seven years in Japan. Upon her return to the States she served as Traffic Referee with Judge W. Sanders in Baton Rouge until Judge Sanders was elected to the Supreme Court of Louisiana. She was instrumental in the organization and continuation of the Youth Council in East Baton Rouge Parish, Louisiana.

Was Jean Lafitte Truly a Pirate?

JEAN LAFITTE
This is probably the only authentic picture of Jean Lafitte (photo furnished by Gilbert J. Fortier, Jr.)

WAS JEAN LAFITTE TRULY A PIRATE?

Jean Lafitte, who operated mainly at Barataria during the early part of the nineteenth century, can hardly be compared to the early pirates of the Gulf Coast. Stanley C. Arthur in his biography calls him a "Gentleman Rover." There is no doubt that he was very clever, cunning, and quite well educated. But Walker Gilbert, deputy surveyor under Thomas Freeman, surveyor of Public Lands in Mississippi and Louisiana for the United States government, referred to him as the "most base and daring (bandit) ever known in any country on earth." Gilbert, who was stationed at Donaldsonville, had appealed to Freeman to interest the Federal government in capturing the banditti at Barataria. This was in 1814, just previous to Lafitte's spell of good fortune, which was to exonerate him, and make him a hero in addition. General Sir Edward Pakenham (in the War of 1812) left Jamaica early in December, 1814, with his fleet to capture New Orleans, and upon his arrival (December 10) wrote Jean Lafitte, who had, with his brother Pierre, built up a lucrative privateering business, and commanded a formidable force of rough men, inviting him to join forces with the British, offering him the rank of captain, and protection for his buccaneering enterprise. Jean pretended to be favorable to the offer but immediately sent the letter of the English gentleman to Governor Claiborne, along with an offer to aid in the defense of New Orleans. General Andrew Jackson had arrived at New Orleans on December 2, and this correspondence was referred to him. He promptly accepted Lafitte's offer, and found him to be very helpful not only in planning the defense for the Battle of New Orleans but also in the field with his men, who proved to be brave and able soldiers.

Perhaps had it not been for Lafitte and his men the British could not have been defeated by January 8, 1815, and the struggle would have been long and costly. When Governor Claiborne offered a $500 reward for the capture of Lafitte that cocky magnate retaliated by offering $1,500 for the person of the governor. New Orleans thought it funny but Claiborne didn't appreciate the joke.

We are not especially concerned here with the legal aspects of piracy but with the character of persons to whom the name of "pirate" has been applied. In 1605 a den of pirates, very similar to the haven of the Lafitte Brothers of Barataria, was discovered at Broad Haven on the coast of Ireland. An Irish gentleman of the name of Cormac was living there in great splendor but the source of his wealth was a mystery. Sir William Monson, who had been sent to hunt pirates in the Shetlands, found that his castle was headquarters for the pirates of that area, and their captains were living with his daughters (or women who said they were his daughters). Merchants of London and Galway flocked to buy the goods he had to sell at very low prices. Monson put the whole family under the gallows, and frightened them into turning King's evidence. In this way he was able to round up all the pirates of the Irish coast. He claimed that he had cleared the coast of them entirely. But they came back.

It is doubtful that Lafitte ever robbed a ship himself or that he ever committed murder personally. Probably the Irish gentleman Cormac didn't either but they were both as guilty as the pirates whose plunder they sold. And the merchants who purchased the plundered goods at bargain prices (or at any price) could not be considered to be of high integrity. It is said that Lafitte sold slaves as well as merchandise, and the merchants of New Orleans did not hesitate to buy whatever he had to sell.

After Lafitte and his cohorts of Barataria were pardoned by the President (at the request of General Jackson) he became a dramatic figure in New Orleans. Jean and his brothers were without funds. Their warehouses at Grand Terre had been looted, and their ships had been seized. Creditors were demanding payment. But the city was under martial law. General Jackson was in absolute power. When the La Courriere de La Louisiane published an unsigned statement advising the people to cease obeying Jackson's military tribunal, and appeal to the courts of law, he ordered the author Louis Louaillier arrested. This man's attorney, Louis Morel, procured a writ of habeas corpus from United States Judge Dominic A. Hall (born in England), the jurist who sat in judgement on the Lafittes. Jackson tore up the writ and ordered the arrest of Judge Hall. But only a few days later a letter from President Madison arrived announcing that the treaty between the United States and England had been ratified. The war had come to an end. Jackson was no longer military governor of New Orleans. Louaillier was released from custody, Judge Hall was restored to his post, and Jackson was summoned before him for contempt of court. The judge refused to grant him a trial by jury, as he requested, and simply fined him $1,000. Jackson immediately paid the fine and walked out of the courtroom. The people of New Orleans gathered up the amount of the fine among themselves, and gave it to Jackson. But he refused to accept it, and requested that it be given to the families of soldiers who had been killed or wounded in the war.

Apparently Jean and his brother Pierre felt that the government had been ungrateful to them for the assistance they rendered in the Battle of New Orleans, and they became spies for the Intelligence Service of the Spanish Cortez and Crown, a body seeking to introduce the Holy Inquisition into Louisiana.

This employment was not lucrative enough for the Lafitte Brothers, and they moved the establishment from Barataria to Galveston. They still acted as undercover agents for Spain. But when Jean attempted to set himself up as governor of Galveston, he was driven away. Although he had won glory at the Battle of New Orleans, he seemed impelled to follow his natural bent: to plunder, to steal, to lie, and to cheat. He was a colorful character, of that there is no doubt, but with his high intellectual capacity, his cunning genius, and his personal magnetism, he could have risen to a place of eminence in the industrial or political world. Stanley C. Arthur has written a splendid biography of Jean Lafitte, published by Harmanson's Book and Art Store, New Orleans, La.

EXAMPLE OF A TRUE PIRATE
SIR HENRY MORGAN

If there is a heaven, and there should be, it is the abode of the souls of many men, women and children of seventeenth century South America, who begged for their lives innocently but were compelled to suffer such torture that they implored God to let them die, and they died. Likewise, if there is a hell, and there should be, Sir Henry Morgan's soul is there, seething in its gloom, beside Hernando Cortez and Francisco Pizarro. Henry Morgan, a Welshman, was the son of Robert Morgan of Llanrhymny in Glamorganshire. He was born in 1635. He is said to have been kidnapped at Bristol and sold as a slave at Barbados. Or he was "sold for his passage to the New World," after the fashion of those days — i.e., he agreed to pay for his passage in service on the other side, where labor was in great demand. By whatever means he arrived in the Americas, he became a genius in murder and robbery. Although Spain was not at war with England at the time (1666), the British government nevertheless encouraged piratical excursions against Spanish merchant ships but did not encourage the raiding of towns and the unbelievable cruelties practiced by Henry Morgan. Still the British, to their everlasting discredit, did nothing to prevent it.

From Barbados Morgan made his way to Jamaica, and there found a vessel being fitted out for a buccaneering expedition. He slipped aboard, and remained on that vessel as a subordinate during several profitable voyages but he was born to command, and, having a good sum of (stolen) money in his pocket, soon proposed to some of the crew that they purchase a vessel for their own account. This was promptly done, and he was naturally made commander-in-chief.

His first voyage was eminently successful. Having raided the towns of the coast of Mexico, he returned to Jamaica to dispose of his plunder. How many men, women, and children he murdered on this expedition is not known but it is certain that he did not spare any who opposed him. In a tavern in Jamaica, while drinking wine, which was his habit, he met a pirate, whose name was Mansvelt, known as a ship robber of daring and ability. This man, having already noticed the quantity of loot Morgan had captured, instantly offered to appoint him a chief officer in his squadron. Morgan accepted. Mansvelt had a fleet of fifteen vessels, and he and Morgan set out to sea with a crew of several hundred men. They went first to the Island of St. Catherine, where there was a Spanish garrison. There they took the soldiers prisoners, and put the fort in the hands of a company of around a hundred of their own men, with a Frenchman, Le Sieur Simon, in command. It was Mansvelt's intention to make himself ruler of this island, and with this in view he left a good number of slaves there to cultivate the plantations, which he had seized and whose owners he had murdered. He was certain that the British government (under Charles II) would not object to this. The fleet sailed away from St. Catherine, expecting to return and gather the products of the plantations. After raiding the towns on the coast of Costa Rica, murdering many innocent people, they made their way back to St. Catherine, and found an ample supply of provisions for their ships, which the slaves had produced. After several weeks of debauchery they loaded their ships and sailed for Jamaica but as the governor there did not wholly approve of their acts, they sailed on to Tortuga, and there Mansvelt fell ill, and died. Morgan then took full charge of the fleet.

Meantime the Spaniards had taken St. Catherine away from the pirates who had been left there to operate the plantations, and Morgan, sorely disappointed, decided to plunder the coast of Cuba, which was considered a rich territory. He now had twelve vessels and nearly a thousand men. His plan was to attack Havana at midnight, for the inhabitants, taken by surprise, would have scarcely a chance to defend themselves. As this cowardly assault was carried out, a Spanish prisoner, on board one of Morgan's ships, swam ashore to warn the people of the impending danger. They were terrified, and ran as fast as possible to whatever place they could find to hide their valuables, and to save their lives, for they had been informed that Morgan was a man of no mercy, that he was brutal beyond belief, and would slay a child for a trinket as soon as he would swat an insect that annoyed him.

A clear example of Henry Morgan's cruelty is given in "The Story of America," by Hamilton W. Mobie. When he captured the city of Panama he immediately seized two magnificent Catholic churches, eight monasteries, two hundred warehouses, and all the residences of the richest inhabitants.

Those suspected of hiding some of their treasures were put under his usual tortures in order to compel them to give up all they possessed. Many of them were burned alive, others had their eyes dug out, ears and nose cut off, arms dislocated, and others were subjected to unheard-of barbarities. Morgan then went away with his booty, composed of precious metals, jewelry, merchandise, livestock, and six hundred prisoners.

His fleet sailed on to a deserted island not far away to divide the loot. Although these pirates had taken everything of value that could be found, and this was reputed to be a rich country, the booty, when its value was computed, amounted to approximately fifty thousand dollars. Apparently the early inhabitants of the colonies were not after all very wealthy. They were however new in the land and just beginning to build their towns and cities. This Morgan didn't understand, for he constantly tortured them, believing that they were hiding treasures, which in fact did not exist.

Being disappointed with the small amount he procured from his recent plundering expedition, he announced to his crew that he intended to attack Puerto Velo, a city of three thousand inhabitants, located not far from the city of Panama. He said that he was resolved to sack the whole city. But his men cautioned him that this city was protected by a company of three hundred soldiers, and had two strong forts, which guarded every ship that came into the harbor. "If we are few in number we are bold in heart," he replied, "and the fewer we are the greater will be each man's share of the plunder." This statement encouraged the men to proceed.

Morgan was familiar with this area. He anchored his ships at the mouth of a river approximately twenty-five miles from Puerto Velo. Leaving only a few men to guard the vessels, he and his force went up the river in canoes to a point within five miles of the city. Here they landed and traveled on foot along an Indian trail, which ran through a thick forest. It was midnight, and, as they came within sight of the lights of the fort they marched at a slower pace, for they expected resistance. But none came. The soldiers were sound asleep; so were the inhabitants of the city.

As they reached a main street of the city they came upon a guard pacing his beat leisurely. Several of them pounced upon him, and fetched him to Morgan, who questioned him at length concerning the troops of the city, and threatened to kill him instantly unless he gave correct answers. The frightened fellow gave him the information he sought, and the pirates then advanced into the city.

Their first act was to surround the fort. It was still dark, and Morgan sent the following message to the chief officer:

"If you yield at once, your lives shall be saved. But if there is the least resistance, or any delay, I will cut to pieces every individual within the fort. Not one shall escape."

The published account of what followed is unbelievable. Morgan could not have been so capable, nor could the Spaniards have been so stupid as to let him subdue them so completely. It is said that the commandant of the castle (or fort) paid no heed to his threats but immediately opened fire. Then the governor, having been apprised of what was happening, called out all his forces to defend the city. But the pirates had broken down the gates leading to the castle, and the sleeping soldiers had been speedily overpowered. Although the garrison had opened fire, Morgan did not lose a single man. He made all the soldiers prisoners, and drove them into a room next to a powder magazine. Then he laid "a slow match," applied the torch, and with his gang retired to a safe distance. There were a few moments of silence. Then came a roar as if ten thousand thunders had struck at once. Every one of the inmates perished beneath its ruins. This could have been Henry Morgan's story, for he was a braggart and a liar. But he knew nothing of a match in 1670 or at any time in his life, for the friction match was not invented until 1827. He probably had a piece of inflammable resinous wood, known as torchwood, found in the tropics. But how he adroitly placed this torch to blow up the powder magazine only after he and his men had retired to a safe distance is something to ponder over. Why did the explosion, which was "like a volcanic eruption," not injure any of his men? They could not have gone very far away from applying the torch.

The inhabitants were terrified, and went about burying their treasures. The governor, who was so far unhurt, attempted to organize the citizens to defend the town but they were in such a frenzy as to be useless. Only a few men had the courage to resist. They could not hinder the pirates, although they tried hard to protect the nuns and priests, whom they held in reverence. Morgan took them prisoners, and many of the priests were shot while they prayed and begged God to save the inhabitants from the wrath of this vicious man. The people implored the governor to surrender, for they preferred to give up their valuables rather than submit to torture. But he refused, saying: "No, never. I'd rather die like a soldier than be hanged like a coward." He made an unfortunate decision, for, covered with wounds, he was at last killed, his mangled body left in the street. His wife and children had begged him on bended knees to surrender. Morgan was now master of the city, and the nuns, mothers and maidens were at the mercy of the pirates, who promptly took advantage of them.

Morgan and his pirates remained in the city for more than two weeks, still torturing the inhabitants to compel them to reveal where their treasures were hidden. But they had nothing left to hide; these robbers had taken all.

Juan Perez de Guzman, governor of Panama, an able general, who had won many victories in the Spanish service, sent Morgan a note saying: "If you do not immediately withdraw, with your ships, from Puerto Velo, I will march upon you with resistless force. You shall receive no quarter. Every man shall be put to death." Morgan replied as follows: "If you do not send me one hundred and eighty thousand dollars in gold, I will lay every building in Puerto Velo in ashes; I will blow up the forts; and I will put every captive I have to the sword, man, woman and child." The governor of Panama did not send the money, and it was too late to send his army to rescue the people of Puerto Velo, for the pirates, having taken everything of value in Puerto Velo, sailed away, and landed on the coast of Cuba, where they divided the loot, which amounted to three hundred thousand dollars. With this infamous wealth they headed for Jamaica, and upon arriving there proceeded to squander it. The people, high and low, it is said, opened their doors to them, and praised them loudly for their generosity and courage, but in a few weeks when thed had squandered all, the doors were closed in their faces. Either Morgan was in some ways an irresponsible fool or he derived satisfaction only from torturing human beings and wealth was not actually his objective. His pleasure in robberies was not so much in the treasure as in witnessing the suffering of the people from whom he took it.

Henry Morgan's expedition in piracy is a disgrace to the civilization of the seventeenth century, and certainly a disgrace to the British crown, for any decent governing body would have prohibited the murder and torture of helpless people who were not practicing aggression but living in a new land, suffering the travail of the pioneer, in the hope that they could establish comfortable homes.

Morgan did not stop when he had plundered the cities along the coast of the Caribbean Sea but continued along the west coast of South America. To relate further the details of his murder, torture, and robbery there, would be merely to repeat what has already been said. His method was the same wherever he went. He was always eminently successful in overcoming the forces that protected the communities, and always made himself master of the situation, whatever it happened to be. He was without a doubt a genius in strategy.

Juan Perez de Guzman said in a note to him: "It is a pity that a man of so much courage is not in the service of a good prince." It is not likely, however, that a "great and good prince" would have found any use for Henry Morgan's special talents.

Finally the pirates fought among themselves. Morgan, having cheated the members of his expedition of the fair share of the spoils, escaped with a few ships to Jamaica, leaving the rest to get home as best they could. Upon his arrival he received "thanks of the governor" (it is difficult to understand for what!) but a treaty had been signed between Spain and England, and Morgan was ordered home to answer for his conduct. He was arrested and ordered to stand trial. He was however successful in gaining the favor of Charles II, who appointed him lieutenant governor of Jamaica. He was knighted upon leaving England. There was one man among officials of the British government, Lord Vaughan, the governor of Jamaica, who looked with horror upon Morgan's abominable scenes of cruelty and debauchery, and had him suspended from all his employments. He was reinstated to his place in the council in 1788, shortly before his death at the age of fifty-three. He came of a rough family with low moral standards. His brother, Captain Charles Morgan, was a terrible ruffian, and so was his kinsman, Colonel Byndlos, both pirates, famous for their cruelties, brawls, and drunken orgies.

KEEL BOAT ON THE MISSISSIPPI

Types of Crafts on the Old River Front

The workers in maritime commerce of very early New Orleans were accustomed to the flatboats, the luggers and the schooners which carried the cargo of commerce up and down the Mississippi, and the smacks or cutters for the coastal trade, and the brigs and brigantines which handled the overseas commerce. As these carriers were the only means of transportation, they constituted the largest industry in the city. A great number of workers were required to operate even a small boat, and many more were required to unload her, for every package had to be lifted and carried by hand. The flatboats were, of course, propelled by manpower when they moved upstream, and rowing against the Mississippi current was very hard work. In fact, moving upstream was so difficult that, in many instances, the operators sold their boats for a low price when they reached New Orleans and made the return journey by stagecoach or on horseback.

The flats, before 1825, when the steamboats began to handle the bulk of the river cargo, carried a tremendous tonnage in hauling furs from the upper Mississippi to New Orleans for export, and they carried upstream also a great quantity of food, clothing and every conceivable item for the inhabitants of the Mississippi Valley. They also accommodated passengers, for they were the chief means of transportation. There were trails cut through the woods, and a few roads, but overland traveling was extremely difficult. These floating crafts, generally called "flatboats," were of many types, each with a special name, but they were all in the same service and were equally uncomfortable and hard to operate. Among the various types were the arks, the broad horns, the mackinaws, the sleds, the keelboats, the ordinary rafts, and the real flats.

The heavy keel boats, most of them 18 feet wide and 70 feet long, presented problems on upstream trips, for they carried as much as seventy tons of cargo, in addition to passengers and crew.

The most common method of ascending the river was by poling. The poles were equipped with a wooden crutch on one end and an iron shoe on the other. Ten to twenty men on both sides of the boat set the iron shoes against the bottom of the river and the crutches against the shoulders, thus forcing the boat along. It was necessary to float the boat close to the shore. Sometimes ropes of five hundred to a thousand feet long were used to propel the boat by men on shore. Most of the boats were, however, operated by oars, but some were equipped with paddle wheels operated by hand or horsepower. The paddle wheel was a very modern affair on the Mississippi in 1800, and those who used it were not considered very practical. The old-timers in the barge business looked down on them, and gave them the laugh as they passed them by. A good flatboat with 24 or 26 oars could sail ahead of any mechanically propelled craft of that day.

When Ulloa sent an expedition to the Illinois country in 1767 two flatboats were provided, each of 24 oars, and it was stated in the instructions issued that there should be five or seven men always resting so that shifts may be made in the labor. That work was fatiguing in the first five or six days, as the men were not accustomed to it, and did not know how to row; however, they later became skillful and dextrous at it.

These two flatboats provided Ulloa for his expedition were in charge of a French officer, Guido du Fosatton, and among others to look after his comfort and safety were: Donald Duralde, an interpreter; Don Julio Valleau, a surgeon; Jose Maria Suares, a carpenter; Joseph Balboa, a bricklayer; and several others of various trades. Each one received pay equal to his customary earnings in his particular trade. The interpreter, Duralde, is said to have understood the Indian language as well as French, Spanish, and English.

Keel Boat

In the case of flats of a lighter type, oars were more commonly used both to increase the speed of the craft going down stream and to propel it laboriously upstream irrespective of what method of propulsion was used; the ascent was a long and tedious journey. From three to five months were required to move a boat from New Orleans to Louisville, Kentucky, depending upon the current.

The flatboats held sway on the Mississippi for a long time, and the steamboats, when they came, were a long time putting them out of business.

The first steamboat, the **New Orleans,** captained by Nicholas Roosevelt, arrived at the City on January 10, 1812, but as late as 1816 among the arrivals reported at New Orleans, there were only six steamboats as against 1,881 flats and barges.

The steamboat business progressed slowly for a few years, for in 1811 Edward Livingston, a brilliant and crafty lawyer, who settled in New Orleans about the time of the Louisiana Purchase, and won fame as counsel for the Lafitte brothers, persuaded the Legislature of the Orleans territory to grant sole steamboat privileges on the Mississippi to him and Robert Fulton for 18 years, effective January 1, 1812, with the condition that for every boat of 70 tons burthen constructed by them within three years they would have an extension for four years beyond the 18-year period. Any person employing a steamboat in the specified waters was to forfeit and pay to Livingston and Fulton the sum of $5,000. No great protest was made at first, for there were not many steamboats built, and few were trying to get into the business because of the monopoly. But in 1814 Captain Henry Shreve built the steamboat ENTERPRISE at Brownsville, Kentucky, and came down to New Orleans with ammunition for General Jackson. He remained at this port after the war, operating his boat up and down the river from New Orleans to the Gulf, using it chiefly as a tow for vessels coming into this harbor, a service greatly needed. Later he began to make trips north of New Orleans, ignoring the Livingston-Fulton privileges, but Edward Livingston attached the ENTERPRISE. Captain Shreve carried the matter to the United States Supreme Court, which ruled the monopoly illegal, and declared the river open to all the people of the country. It is stated in Henry Rightor's **Standard History of New Orleans** that in 1860 Captain Bruce of Texas, operating the steamboat DISPATCH, lost $1,500 because he was prohibited at New Orleans from taking a return cargo of sugar, and that he protested this monopoly; and it is stated also in this same book that a steamer arrived from Wheeling with a flag carrying the motto, "Our friends shall not withhold what we have wrested from our enemies." — in reference to the Livingston-Fulton claim. Livingston died in 1836, and Fulton died in 1815. Moreover, the monopoly was granted for 18 years (from January 1, 1812), and so it expired by limitation in 1830 — or if it was extended for four years because of the construction of another boat, the franchise would have ended long before 1860. As a matter of fact, Captain Thomas P. Leathers was operating the steamboat **Princess** in the Yazoo trade as early as 1841, and not many years later his boats ran between Natchez and New Orleans. Surely this courageous captain, who defied General Butler, and refused to sign the "Oath of Allegiance" in order to carry the mails, and got his way, would not have stood for the Livingston-Fulton monopoly.

In 1821, however, 287 steamboats arrived at this port and only 1,225 flats. But four years later the flatboats were hardly used at all. They were as scarce as the T-model Ford is today. There were still some crafty farmers of the Illinois territory who built barges, loaded them with produce and floated down to New Orleans, where they sold the produce and the barge, too. In those days, anything could be sold in New Orleans, which was about the busiest harbor in America — or it was at least the harbor which handled the greatest variety of items. These flatboats and steamboats transported cargo from all parts of the interior for export, and by 1821, when the population of New Orleans was only about 30,000, the exports from this port reached the figure of $16,000,000. For the transportation of this vast cargo for coastwise and overseas destination the river bank at New Orleans was lined with brigs, brigantines, smacks, schooners, cutters, etc. These vessels tied up wherever they could find a place, usually opposite what is now the French Quarter, but as the steamboats pulled up with steam in their glory, the flatboats, now fallen into disrepute, found a lonely berth on the American side of the city, usually along South Front Street. In time, there were definite regulations, and the steamboats docked only on the upper side of Canal Street and on the lower side of Customhouse Street. Ocean vessels docked below this area, and the flatboats and barges above.

It seems that for a while (about 1826) the flatboats were out of the running. From 600 to 800 steamboat arrivals were reported at New Orleans, and no flats. But after this time the cargo transported on the Mississippi increased so rapidly that the steamboats could not handle the traffic, and flatboat operation became profitable. In 1832 more than 4,000 flats descended the river, and in 1845 the arrivals at the New Orleans river front were recorded as 2,500 steamboats and 2,700 flats of all types. (It is doubtful that there were 2,500 steamboats arriving at this time, regardless of statements in some government records and copied by writers of history). There was then to be seen at the wharves of the city every type of craft known to the maritime industry, including ocean steamers, river packets, flats, luggers, brigs, brigantines, clipper ships, cutters, smacks, and fishing boats of every classification.

The **Golden Era** of the steamboat may be reckoned between 1845 and 1900. In 1820, for instance, there were only 73 steamboats operating in "Western waters" (the west was then the Mississippi Valley). In 1828 there were only 181 (some records show 698, which is apparently incorrect), and in 1842 there were about 450 (other records say 705). Yet it is reported in some government records, according to Harold Sinclair, in his book, **The Port of New Orleans,** that there were 2,500 steamboat arrivals at New Orleans in 1845. It is hardly possible that 2,050 steamboats were built in two years. Mr. Sinclair, too, doubts the accuracy of this figure.

Steamboat "EDWARD J. GAY" at Dock, New Orleans. This was one of the finest boats on the River around 1860.

As late as 1852 Louisiana had only 63 miles of railroad in operation, and so the steamboats had virtually no competition. But as the railroads were developed, shipping trade increased, and there was enough for both rail and water carriers to thrive. Trade continued to increase, but the railroads, offering faster service, and spreading their lines to every village across the country, took it all. The magnificent steamboats, once the pride of the river, were now too slow.

The steamboat operating companies, which had grown rich in the trade, were gradually compelled to liquidate, because they could no longer operate at a profit. Many of them, however, were able to survive the railroad competition until well into the twentieth century. Such boats as the **Ohio,** (the largest on the river), the **Governor Shelby,** the **Aetna,** and the **Kentucky,** which plied between New Orleans and Louisville, from 1816 to 1820, had made their owners rich. They had long hauls, high freight and passenger rates, and cheap labor. The later boats, such as the **Natchez,** the **T. P. Leathers,** the **Robert E. Lee,** the **Chalmette,** and the **Valley Queen,** and others found keen competition in their own trade as well as among the railroads. Still they made money, but it was not so easy, and the time came when their whistles sounded no more along the banks of "Old Man River."

EARLY STRIKES ON THE RIVER

On November 24, 1890, at Cinclare Plantation, Brusly Landing, Louisiana, a special correspondent for the Sunday Inter-Ocean (newspaper) of Chicago, Illinois, wrote an article about the New Orleans river front, which was published in that paper on November 30 of the same year. The article was entitled "Up and Down the Mississippi," and told of the scenes along the levee at New Orleans during the season of sugar and cotton and about the "stevedore strike," on which he frequently quoted Captain Thomas P. Leathers, who gave his opinion freely.

The long warehouses were full of sugar, and outside there were "acres of molasses barrels and bales of cotton." The "pitiful lack of a belt line of railway about the city" made the movement of freight, "sweeping the city like a flood," slow and cumbersome. It was said that the hauling of cotton cost an average of $4.00 a bale, and that this might be reduced to about one quarter through the medium of a belt line railway; but now there was entirely too much grass growing between the tracks in the Crescent City.

The demand for labor was great, the supply inadequate, and the "expensive-shouldered son of Ham" was taking advantage of the situation. It was complained that the day crew, well fed, and with pockets full of money, left the boats as soon as they landed, for they did not purpose to "tote freight" when there was pleasure waiting. They slept on the barrels of molasses and on the bales of cotton, and as long as their cash lasted they didn't give a hang whether the boats were unloaded or not. The steamboat operators tried what they termed "alien labor," but they preferred the Negro with all his grievous faults. The Negro was criticized not only for his indifference to work, but also for the way he "invested his money"; he ate and drank to his full satisfaction and sometimes bought a "flaming flannel shirt," but other than this he had nothing to show for his earnings. The writer for the **Sunday Inter-Ocean** considered, therefore, that the Negro, in view of his high rate of pay, was a "poor investor."

But the Negro didn't think that his wage was quite high enough to permit him to set himself up in a comfortable home or to lead a completely respectable life or even to provide all that he actually needed. Lacking this, he spent most of his leisure hours at the "dram-shop" on the levee, the door of which was always open, for here he could forget the injustice heaped upon him. And so the special correspondent of the

Sunday Inter-Ocean said: (as he viewed the river front) "Great bells are clanging; some boats are backing into the stream half loaded for the up trip; others have pulled tarpaulins over their freight to leave it on land, a melancholy monument to their inability to get it loaded. A labor strike is imminent."

Captain Leathers, "the Nestor of the Mississippi," now nearly 80, with a broad-brimmed hat covering his silver locks, an old-fashioned ruffle adorning his bosom, was standing on the hurricane deck of his steamer bemoaning the "degeneracy of the times." He referred to his favorite subject — how Captain Eads had caused overflows along the Mississippi in building the jetties at the mouth of the river — and then he took up the question of the strike. There was no use in trying to work a Negro when he had plenty, he thought, and, after a few more very uncomplimentary remarks concerning the longshoremen (referred to frequently as stevedores) he added that "monopoly is the curse of the age."

The freight kept piling up. There was no picketing as in the case of a "beef" today; some men were working and some were not. Something had to be done. There was no organized labor union with which to deal, but there were many longshoremen urging their companions to lay off; that is, not to work unless a higher wage was offered. Meanwhile, a foreman, Billy Duke, with a small voice and a big stick and a vocabulary of very choice curse words, was getting all that was possible out of those who would work. Finally, the steamboat operators could stand it no longer; they were losing money, and so, feeling that ruination was no worse one way than another, they took a chance and offered the crew $90. a month. That was considered a good wage in 1890. For the price of bacon was 24 cents a pound as compared to 77 cents today. Anyway the crew was satisfied, and boats with as many as 9,300 bales of cotton were unloaded — which was too much cotton for an average boat according to the insurance companies, who advised that 3,500 bales would be enough. But the steamboats were in business to make money.

All the while Captain Leathers, standing in the rays of electric lights, was thinking of the Golden Era of steamboating on the Mississippi, when such boats as the BALTIC, the LEE, the NATCHEZ, and the DIANA were the fliers on the river between New Orleans and Louisville, traveling a distance of 1,382 miles, always racing and keeping within sight of one another. The race between ROBERT E. LEE and the NATCHEZ, in June 1870, had excited more interest in New Orleans and up and down the river than any other contest on the river or on the ocean within the memory of men of the times. It is said that a billion dollars in stakes changed hands. The NATCHEZ, with Captain Thomas P. Leathers, had made the run of 1,278 miles, from New Orleans to St. Louis, in 3 days, 21 hours and 58 minutes. The LEE, with Captain John W. Cannon commanding, carrying no freight or passengers, and taking her fuel from boats en route without stopping, reduced the NATCHEZ time 33 minutes. The NATCHEZ made the run in the regular way, but was grounded and lost six hours — otherwise she would have won the race.

EASY MONEY

Almost up to the twentieth century the levee was the busiest place in New Orleans, and, in a way, the most corrupt. Here confidence men lured unsuspecting merchants into their shady deals and swindled them; here the laborers shot dice, and men of wealth made bets on boat races, markets or anything uncertain; here the gamblers spotted their prey as they boarded the river packets, and the thieves of the river front stole bags of sugar, coffee and rice, which they sold to dishonest grocers in the city, mainly on Girod Street, and sometimes on Gallatin Street, where it is said no legitimate business ever existed. This is not to say that Decatur St., Front St., North and South Peters Streets had in any way a saintly reputation, for they, too, supported places which were frequented by all types of swindlers and gamblers from various parts of the world, and quite frequently by such notorious gamesters as Jimmy Fitzgerald, Charles Starr, Dick Hargraves, John Powell, George M. White, and others too numerous to mention. But the few mentioned here were not penny-ante gamblers. They were those who spotted the rich and gullible sugar planters who took passage on the steamboats, and trimmed them in a big way. For instance, Jimmy Fitzgerald won almost enough money to live like a nabob, except that he kept only three slaves to attend his person — a nabob keeps about ten times that many. But in his dress he was the Beau Brummel of New Orleans. He left the city after a good haul, and went to California, where he killed two women in a fight, and was heard of no more on the steamboats of the Mississippi. It is said that "Colonel" Charles Starr's winnings were sufficient to enable him to purchase several plantations along the Mississippi, but nobody ever knew exactly where they were. He was a man who liked to brag. He did, however, acquire a considerable fortune by his "skill" at card-playing, but through recklessness, especially in trying to break the Faro banks in New Orleans and St. Louis, he lost it. It is not clear whether the "Colonel" killed himself or died of starvation. In his book, "The French Quarter," Herbert Asbury says that he entered a restaurant and ordered a meal, but when the manager demanded payment in advance he walked out. An hour later, having pawned his overcoat, he came back to the place and ordered up to the amount he had received, which was five dollars. When the meal was served he carefully turned every dish upside down on the table. That night he died. It is not stated how. Dick Hargraves won approximately two million dollars (from 1840 to about 1880) in river front gambling houses and on the river packets. He first found out about "easy picking" on the river when he won thirty thousand dollars on one trip from a sugar planter. He was a clever man, and had he devoted himself to some legitimate business he may have done quite well, for, beginning as a bartender, he acquired a good education and very elegant manners. During the War Between the States he enlisted in the Union Army, and became a major.

John Powell, a rich and distinguished appearing gentleman, having won about fifty thousand dollars from Jules Devereaux, a prosperous sugar planter, several months later engaged a young Englishman in a game and won eight thousand dollars from him, but since this young man came on deck the next morning and shot himself, Mr. Powell refrained from gambling for a year. This does not, however, prove that he had a conscience, for he now had close to sixty thousand cash in his pockets, and he may have felt like taking it easy for a while, for gambling for a living is hard work. Whether a man is winning or losing the strain is terrific.

Major George M. White was perhaps the only steamboat gambler of any fame who did not meet with a bad ending. Born in 1805, he began his gambling career in New Orleans in 1825, and retired comfortably well off in 1887. Thus after sixty-two years of living by games of chance, except for a certain income of four hundred dollars a week which he received for running a faro bank in New Orleans, he made his home in California, and died there at the age of ninety-five.

Gambling was by no means confined to the elite, nor to the steamboats, but was carried on in every tavern or coffeehouse or dram-shop on the river front. Dice games were more popular on the levee and in the shops of the river front. Poker, seven up, faro, the shell game, and blackjack were popular on the steamboats. Many a sugar planter arrived home with a year's profit lost on the way in a game of cards, but he had good credit and made it back the next season if the weather was favorable and the cane crop good. Perhaps he had only to deny his family a trip to Europe or a summering resort; but the longshoreman who lost his week's wages lost all he had, and his family suffered for want of food. But such was the way of the river front.

It is not unlikely that in some cases the stealing on the river front was the result of workers losing their week's wages at dice and trying to replenish their cash by lifting a few bags of sugar and selling them at a low price.

John Law and Paper Money

New Orleans, having been transferred (without its consent) from one nation to another three times in the course of its history, was not without difficult periods in the matter of finances and mediums of exchange. First Louis XIV transferred the commerce or trade of Louisiana (1712) to a wealthy banker, Antoine de Crozat, for a period of fifteen years, and gave him complete control of the finances of the colony. Because of his greed, this project was a dismal failure. In order to force the colonists to trade with him, Crozat allowed only his own vessels to enter the ports of the colony. And he fixed prices on all merchandise. He "bought low and sold high." As a result a great smuggling trade sprang up, and his venture became unprofitable, not only because of the smuggling business but people refused to pay his prices, and got along without items they would normally buy. Finally he gave up his charter, for the people openly rebelled against his inordinate tyranny and outrageous prices. They pillaged his storehouse and killed one of the men in charge of it.

Then came the redoubtable John Law with his "Mississippi Scheme." He was a Scots economist, who had studied mathematics and considered himself an authority on commerce and political economy. But he was, at least when young, more a fop than a scholar. He gambled and drank, until in 1694 in a love intrigue he fought a duel with a man of the name of Beau Wilson, whom he killed, and was condemned to death but escaped to Holland. This is the man who, as head of the "Company of the West," was to have (in the interest of France) the exclusive monopoly of the trade of Louisiana for twenty-five years. He had several years before attempted to sell his scheme to Louis XIV, who declined to trade with him because he was a Protestant. But when the duke of Orleans became regent of France, Law approached him with his peculiar scheme: to pull France out of debt and bring about prosperity.

Law had the idea that "money is not the result but the cause of wealth," and the best way to increase it was to issue quantities of paper currency properly secured. In his opinion gold or silver had no intrinsic value, and therefore was not real security, while land and/or property of value was actual security. Thus the vast territory of the Mississippi Valley was considered to be splendid backing for paper money.

The duke of Saint-Simon, who was present when Law negotiated with the Regent, said: "I have never comprehended, nor has anybody, I fancy, during all the ages which have elapsed since that in which Abraham, after losing Sarah bought, for ready money, a sepulcher for her and for her children. But Law was a man of system, and of system so deep, that nobody ever could get to the bottom of it, though he spoke easily, well and clearly, but with a good deal of English in his French."

Realizing that as a Protestant he could not succeed with his project in France, Law became a Catholic, and embraced this religion in earnest, although the duke of Saint-Simon said that "Law's wife was not his wife, she came of a good English family, well connected," and bore him two children, a son and a daughter, whom he educated and cared for with great affection. Why he never married this woman is unknown; but she was at least his common law wife.

After the failure of the Mississippi Scheme (or Mississippi Bubble, as it is sometimes called) the people of France were bitter against him, and demanded punitive measures. But he escaped to Venice where he died in 1729, at the age of 59, forgotten and in comparative poverty. He continued to embrace the Catholic religion, and received with piety the last sacraments of the church.

CANAL STREET in 1857. This picture appeared in Ballou's Pictorial of August 1, 1857. The picture was made from the pencil of Mr. Kilburn from a photograph by James Andrews of Nos. 3 and 5 St. Charles Street.

The Company of the Mississippi at first met with glittering success in Louisiana as well as in France but its failure was complete, and brought great distress upon the colonists. Many of them left, and it seemed for a while that New Orleans and all Louisiana would become deserted as a result of unwise commercial and financial policy of the French government. The Regent was not an able man; he was in a sense stupid, and certainly untrustworthy.

After 1720 (about the time the bubble burst) Louisiana continued to use paper money, the value of which fluctuated from time to time. When the Company, which had control of Louisiana, settled up its affairs (in settlement of its debts), a quantity of bonds called "billets de caisse" were issued, and came into general use as currency. But they interfered with the "king's coins" (real money) to such an extent that Governor Perier found it necessary (around 1731) to issue a proclamation in which he fixed the time that these "billets" should cease to be used as currency, and should be withdrawn from circulation. This edict caused a financial crisis, for there were few coins in Louisiana. In 1735 the French Government endeavored to replace the depreciated paper money with pasteboard notes (known as billets de carte), which, it was said, were guaranteed by the government. But the people had little more confidence in "the government" than in the bankrupt companies, and the billets went downward until in 1744, nine years after their issue, they were worth 33¢ on the dollar.

Therefore, if a man sold his corn at $1.00 a bushel and accepted billets in payment at face value, he only got 33¢ a bushel for it. Again the people protested so bitterly that the Council of State called a meeting and decided to call in all the pasteboard notes, and redeem them at 40¢ on the dollar, which was obviously only slightly higher than their current value. Naturally this was not considered a fair settlement. But to make matters worse, instead of paying cash for these "billets de carte" the Council gave drafts on the Treasury of France, and upon turning in these notes or billets the colonists were not paid for them in New Orleans but were given orders on Paris. It was further proclaimed that any billets not presented within two months of the proclamation would be null and void and, therefore, valueless, and could not be accepted in payment of debts. The people were again swindled, as they had been since the settlement of Louisiana.

But Louisiana had to have something as a medium of exchange, whether gold, silver, or paper, and several years later Governor Vaudreuil, on his own responsibility, issued a new paper currency, for no assistance came from France, and the currency in circulation was not sufficient for the growing trade in the colony. This paper money was issued in bills from $4.00 up. (What was back of it is unknown, unless it was the local government.) This plan had been suggested by the Intendant Commissary Michel de la Rouvilliere, and approved by Vaudreuil. But France disapproved of this issue of currency, and ordered all notes retired. The governor was advised that he had no authority to issue paper notes. The notes were so badly printed that many counterfeits were found on the market. A Negro, Joseph, seems to have been responsible for most of them.

There was some improvement in matters of money when Louisiana was transferred to Spain, but not much. A good quantity of silver coins came in from Mexico; not enough, however, to make any great difference in the deplorable money situation. The Spanish government, therefore, issued paper money, known as "liberanza," with no security back of it, and it soon depreciated in value like the rest of the paper money. There was unending difficulty in financing the foreign and local trade of the colony. Foreign and coastwise vessels brought thousands of tons of merchandise into the port every month, and paying for it with money of uncertain value was a serious problem.

Finance and banking in Louisiana had been handled in so hap-hazard a manner that the people were inclined to use products as mediums of exchange, except in exports and imports — such as a dozen eggs for two pounds of sugar, or ten chickens for a ham, or two cows for a horse. It is true that paper money has been in use for centuries but it is backed by some standard commodity of intrinsic value into which it may be converted upon demand. France had nothing back of its paper.

When Louisiana was transferred to Spain there were 7,000,000 livres of paper money in circulation, and the colonists were hopeful that the Spanish government would redeem it at face value. But the French government had established 25 percent as the legal amount of depreciation. The matter was placed before the Spanish governor Ulloa, and he ordered the French notes to be received by the Spanish as well as by the French at the rate of 75 percent of the face value. The colonists were not satisfied, and demanded par for their paper but could not dispose of it even at the discount whereupon Ulloa, as a matter of diplomacy, bought up a large quantity of the French paper at 75¢ on the dollar. He attempted to use this French paper to pay the Spanish troops, giving them one-third in French notes and two thirds in cash. But they refused to accept the paper.

An example of the difficulties encountered in the use of this paper money of uncertain value is given by Jack D. L. Holmes in his biography of Gayoso: "When a young English traveler, Francis Baily came to Natchez in 1797 with a cargo of merchandise, he contracted with the secretary of the government, Joseph Vidal, to buy the entire lot for a stipulated price,

Vidal tendered paper currency to Baily, which the Englishman declined to accept when he learned the certificates generally bore a 12 percent discount in New Orleans where they were redeemed . . . Baily insisted that Vidal pay hard currency."

The case was referred to Governor Gayoso, and he decided that the paper currency commonly in use was legal tender, or money which the law authorizes a debtor to tender and requires a creditor to receive in payment of money obligations — unless, of course, it had been previously specified and agreed that the said debt must be paid in silver or gold. Baily appealed to the governor general Carondelet in New Orleans. But Carondelet upheld Gayoso's decision.

Clearly, under both French and Spanish domination there was no such thing as banking in Louisiana. Both governments constantly fleeced the colonists by issuing paper currency with nothing back of it, and redeeming it at any figure they wished to set. There was just cause for a "Boston tea party," but people were not sufficiently organized for that. Too many of them felt the mother country was still their home.

There was no relief in the matter of money or the mediums of exchange until after the Louisiana Purchase. When Governor Claiborne arrived in Louisiana he found the financial structure of the state in a deplorable condition, and he promptly suggested that a bank should be established. In less than a year (1804) the Louisiana Bank was founded. The capital was to be two million dollars. But the people, having been fleeced so often, were suspicious of this institution, and hesitated to deal with it. Evan Jones was the first president, and Paul Lanusse was made secretary, and the board comprised fifteen members. Although there was manifestly a need for a bank, for trade was growing by leaps and bounds, the United States Secretary of the Treasury severely censured Claiborne for establishing it. It is hard to imagine what objection he could have had, for nearly everybody in Louisiana had signed a petition requesting the governor to establish a bank as soon as possible. Despite the Secretary's objection, the Louisiana Bank seems to have been "formerly" organized (or reorganized) in January of 1805, with Julien Poydras as president, Stephen Zacharie as cashier, James Fitzgerald and John Thibaut as tellers. The directors were: Paul Lanusse, James Pitot, Julien Poydras, Daniel Clark, Michel Fortier, John Loulie, Thomas Harman, Thomas Urquhart, William Donaldson, John F. Merieult, Francois Duplessis, James Garric, John McDonough, John B. Labatut, and Nicholas Girod. These were the most prominent business men of that period.

This bank operated with considerable success. It was in

fact so successful that within a few months after it began operation the United States Bank of Philadelphia opened a branch bank in New Orleans, and made Evan Jones president. The directors were such prominent men as Thomas Callender, John Palfrey, Benjamin Morgan, Whitten Evans, Beverly Chew, John W. Gurley, J. B. Provost, William Brown, Cavalier Jennier, Joseph McNeil, William Kenner, George T. Phillips, and Evan Jones.

These banks naturally issued paper money but although there was a standard commodity of value back of it, and it was as good as gold, the people (except the educated business men and professional men) protested bitterly, for the worthless paper currency was still fresh in their memory. But it was not long before bank notes became generally acceptable.

The Louisiana Bank, however, was poorly managed, and failed in 1819. The stockholders lost only about 12 percent of their investments. Meantime there had been other banks established. They were stronger, with larger capital, and were better managed. The first of these was the Bank of New Orleans, with a capital of $5,000,000, organized in 1811. The first president of this bank was Benjamin Morgan. He was followed by Samuel Packwood, and next by Zenon Cavalier. By this time the sugar crop of Louisiana had become so great as to require a tremendous amount of financing. The planters were constantly in need of capital to manufacture sugar and to improve their property. They had gilt-edge security, and the banks were naturally in the business of lending money. The Louisiana Planters' Bank was organized (1811) especially for the convenience of the agricultural interest of the state. It made a practice of discounting planters' notes and advancing them money for improvement of property and harvesting crops. Banks and branch banks were also established throughout the sugar belt and in the cotton country.

At the outbreak of the Civil War there were no banks in the whole country in better condition or more solid than the eleven banks then existing in New Orleans. When General B. F. Butler was stationed in control of New Orleans he gave the bankers all the trouble his vile imagination could conceive, for he hated every Southerner from the bottom of his soul, and enjoyed inflicting suffering however he could. When Farragut had captured New Orleans the banks sent $4,000,000 in specie to Montgomery or in the hands of the Confederacy, and Butler demanded an explanation, and ordered it returned. But the Confederate authorities refused to do so. The banks of New Orleans sailed on, however, through the war, and they are still sailing splendidly, now insured, and with greater security than ever in the history of the country.

Money, whether in paper or coin, has been a troublesome item from the beginning of history. It is said that Abraham upon the death of his wife wished to give her a sepulcher, and had to purchase a lot, the owner of which demanded that payment be made not in paper notes nor in goods but in silver shekels (400 silver shekels) which was the medium of exchange among the merchants of Hebron. A silver shekel was worth about $10.88. Abraham weighed the shekels out to the owner of the lot, and received the title.

Debasing coinage was also an ancient practice. William I of England placed a bar of silver 11/12 fine, containing ¾ of an ounce troy more than the troy pound of 5760 grains, and declared it to be standard, both in weight and value. As a standard of value the Tower pound was divided into 240 parts, each part to be known as a penny, and for many years only pennies were coined. Finally out of the pound twenty pieces were coined, and were known as shillings, each containing twelve pieces. In time the pound was divided into twelve parts, each part containing twenty pennyweights. But Edward III, finding his government deep in debt, decided that twenty-two shillings be coined from a pound instead of twenty, and in making the new pieces legal tender, he cheated his creditors out of two shillings on every pound, for the new pieces had no value in the market except that which their weight in bullion gave them.

THE OLD NEW ORLEANS MINT

In 1835 Congress authorized the establishment of three branch mints to be located at New Orleans, La., Charleston, S. C., and Dahlonega, Ga. The mint at New Orleans was completed and began operation by 1838. The mint building at New Orleans, the construction of which cost $182,000, was the largest of the three, and is located at the foot of Esplanade Avenue. It is made of fire bricks, granite and iron, and is, therefore, completely fireproof. The capacity of the plant was estimated to be $5,000,000 a month. From 1838 to 1853 there had been expended on the establishment of this mint, including the cost of construction, labor, and machinery, the sum of $778,630. Apparently production fell far short of the estimate of $5,000,000, for it is recorded that during the year ending July 31, 1851, the gold deposits amounted to $8,285,637.14, and the silver deposits to $822,085.25. The gold coinage for the same year was $8,994,000, and the silver coinage $1,050,500.

At the outbreak of the Civil War in 1861 the mint was abandoned, and being unprotected people went through it as they pleased and took anything they could carry away. But in May of 1861 the State of Louisiana took possession of the mint, and coined Confederate money. After the War (1865) an agent of the United States Mint Bureau found (in January) 32 pairs of dies of 1861, complete in all denominations of United States coins, and he immediately destroyed them.

Dr. W. F. Bonzano, melter and refiner of the mint, made the following statement:

"The branch mint at New Orleans, with all its contents, was 'taken in trust' by secession convention in December, 1860, through a committee of the convention, at the head of which was the president of the convention, ex-Governor A. Mouton. The committee called at the mint, ascertained the amount of bullion in the hands of the treasurer, melter, refiner and coiner, and required a special bond for same from each of these officers. A rough settlement was made, and all dies of 1860 were defaced in the presence of all the officers, except Mr. Guirot. By order of the superintendent, coinage was immediately resumed with the new dies of 1861, and continued until the 31st of May, 1861, when a final settlement was made and all bullion transferred to Mr. A. J. Guirot, who had in the meantime been appointed Assistant Treasurer of the Confederate States; at the same time all the United States dies, of whatever description, after careful examination and recognized agreement with the coiner's die account, were, with the consent of the coiner, defaced by the foreman, Mr. John F. Brown, with the assistance of a workman, Mr. Richard Stevenson.

"Under the auspices of the superintendent, treasurer and coiner, design for a Confederate coin was made, and that for half dollars offered by the coiner, accepted, and was executed by an engraver of New Orleans, who produced a die of such high relief as rendered it impracticable for use in a coinage press. The four pieces differed from the United States standard only in the legend. With the exception of these four pieces, no coins of any kind, different from the United States standard, were ever made at the New Orleans mint during the interval from May 31, 1861, to the early part of 1879.

"Another mark in the mint's life was the alleged burning, in June, 1893, of $25,000 in United States paper currency, in bills of various denominations and character, which were deposited in a large tin box in the steel vault connected with the cashier's office, then in charge of Mr. James M. Dowling, who was cashier, appointed by Dr. A. W. Smythe, recent director of the mint, under Harrison's administration. There was some mystery and doubt as to the manner in which this money caught fire, and suspicion falling on Mr. Dowling, he was arrested on a charge of embezzlement, and bound over to await the action of the Federal grand jury; was indicted, tried and prosecuted vigorously and ably by the United States District Attorney, and was acquitted.

"The theory of the defense being, that the wires connected with the electric globe or bulb lighting the vault became overcharged with electricity, causing the bursting of the bulb, which was made of very thin glass, and scattering about the heated glass and carbon, and that the currency was ignited by these fragments, electrical experts testified that such ignition was possible. Mr. Dowling was indicted for embezzlement, a government witness, expert in such matters, testifying that a minute microscopic examination of the ashes of the burnt money, disclosed a sum of original bills amounting to only $1,185, Dowling alleging $25,000 as being in the box."

Method of Operation

The method of working the metal was as follows: Bullion was received in different forms, such as in bricks, dust, washings, bars, old jewelry, plates, spoons, and various other things. These items were called deposits. The depositor on delivering metal to the weigh clerk received a certificate of deposit showing the gross weight of the metal deposited but was not paid until the metal had been refined to ascertain its value.

Having long since discontinued making coins, the mint was given over to the Coast Guard during World War II, and was used as a Federal jail. Finally the Federal Government transferred the building to the State of Louisiana on condition that it be made into a museum. This requirement is being carried out by the Louisiana State Museum, of which Mrs. Peggy Richards is director.

There have been seven mints in the United States since the establishment of the first mint in Philadelphia (1792). But only two mints are operating now; one in Philadelphia, and the other in Denver, Colorado.

New Orleans Becomes Important Port for Importing Bananas and Other Tropical Fruit

One day in 1874 the longshoremen at the New Orleans river front unloaded 250 bunches of bananas from a small merchantship, the Juan C. Meiggs, which had arrived from Colon. They wondered what they were. "Try one," said one of the hands, "they eat them down in the tropics." One of the men plucked a small ripe banana from the bunch, and ate it with gusto, while the others stood by to see what would happen to him. But as the foreman came along he went back to his job and worked hard, as a brave man satisfied with the daring deed he had done. This lot of bananas had been shipped to New Orleans by Minor Cooper Keith on his brother's small steamer, and they were delivered to the French Market and sold as a luxury. The price was high, and the profit was good for the green-grocers. This was the first cargo of what was to become one of America's greatest enterprises, the United Fruit Company, which today has fixed assets of more than $300,000,000.

An energetic man whose vision encircles a hemisphere or the whole world never knows what by-product of his labor may excel his main objective. Mr. Keith, a native of Brooklyn, New York, went to Central America in 1871 to build railroads. Being a man who had a common-sense way of looking into the future, he considered whether his railroads would have enough freight to haul, and in order to make certain that they would he developed a banana-growing business in the nearby territory. But he did not begin his banana-growing project until he had spent four years in Texas and accumulated a small fortune in the cattle business. It was then (in 1871) that he went to Costa Rica to build a railroad from the Atlantic Coast to San Jose, a distance of a hundred miles. It was a costly venture. The disease-infested swamps, which were to be conquered and made not only safe but healthful, had claimed the lives of about 4,000 persons, three of Minor C. Keith's brothers among them. But tragedy did not deter him. He went on building and making plans to develop a banana-growing project. He had already tested the market with 250 bunches, even before he produced any, and now, while waiting for his own crop, he kept this market, and supplied it with approximately 400 bunches a month. He had procured some root stocks from Carl B. Franc, whom he had known for some time, and planted them on the land which he purchased. It is probable that Mr. Franc was the only man of the tropics growing and exporting bananas. He was shipping them to Philadelphia and New York wrapped in tinfoil. They sold in those markets for about a dollar apiece. Bananas suitable for eating did not grow wild, but, as sugarcane were cultivated. The railroad venture progressed despite well-nigh insuperable handicaps, but banana-growing became the largest of Mr. Keith's enterprises. Before the turn of the century he had organized the Tropical Trading and Transport Company, Ltd., and the Columbian Land Company, Ltd., for cultivating bananas on plantations in Costa Rica and Colombia. He also organized the Snyder Banana Company, which held plantations in Panama. All these enterprises were under his management and control.

But growing bananas, irrespective of the quality of the fruit or the abundance of the yield, was not to be profitable unless they could be sold. Nobody knew this better than the far-seeing Mr. Keith. He consigned his crops to Hoadley and Company at New Orleans, a firm operating on a large scale as distributors of this fruit. But this company failed in 1898, and left Mr. Keith holding bills against it for $1,500,000. It happened that at this time the government of Costa Rica held drafts in very large amounts against Mr. Keith, and so he was for a while in a quandary as to what to do in this difficulty. But he had done much for the people of Costa Rica; he had built the first railroad from Puerto Limon to San Jose, and in doing so had brought prosperity to many. The Costa Rican government was aware of this, and it readily offered to lend him the money to tide him over this crisis. Thus, with the cooperation of the banks and the government of Costa Rica, Mr. Keith was able, within two weeks, to return to the United States, and to settle in full with his creditors. This was an achievement which would have been beyond the ability of one who had not proved himself and won the unfailing confidence of the people with whom he had dealt.

The failure of Hoadley and Company was in a way a fortunate incident in the career of Minor C. Keith, for in searching for another agent to handle his fruit, he called upon Andrew W. Preston, president of the Boston Fruit Company, a man of marked business ability who had recently organized the Fruit Dispatch Company in addition to several other subsidiaries already under his control, and as a result of this meeting the United Fruit Company was organized. It was incorporated on March 30, 1899, under the laws of New Jersey, with an authorized capital of $20,000,000, and among its assets were 44 small sea-going vessels. Mr. Preston was elected president, and Mr. Keith was elected vice-president.

The banana business was not new to Mr. Preston. As early as 1870, when a ship captain brought a few bunches of bananas from Kingston, Jamaica, he saw the possibilities of a great trade in that fruit. But he did not have at that time sufficient capital to develop a market. About fifteen years later, however, he persuaded nine other men to put up $2,000 each and join him in an association to promote the banana trade. This enterprise was known as the Boston Fruit Company. The venture was profitable from the beginning, and by 1899 the company owned and controlled seven other fruit distributing agencies: the American Fruit Company, Quaker City Fruit Company, Banes Fruit Company, Buckman Fruit Company, Dominican Fruit Company, Sama Fruit Company, and the Fruit Dispatch Company.

The function of the Fruit Dispatch Company was to distribute the fruit on its arrival in the United States, and today this same agency distributes bananas running into the tens of millions of bunches every year for the United Fruit Company. It is not an easy matter to keep this vast quantity of perishable fruit in good condition on the shelves of the grocery stores throughout this nation, and it may be said that the Fruit Dispatch Company is one of the most perfectly conceived organizations in America.

These two men, Andrew W. Preston and Minor C. Keith, both of unusual ability, went on with their plans, and as problems came they surmounted them, until they built up a great industrial empire, the trade of which extends to every country on earth, but which is centered in America, especially the United States of America. Mr. Preston died in 1924, and Victor M. Cutter, the company's vice-president at that time, was elected president. Mr. Keith remained a director of the company, but was principally occupied as president of the International Railway of Central America, and spent most of his time in Middle America. He died at a great age in 1930.

In 1902, Crawford H. Ellis, a man eminently qualified to steer a great enterprise, was appointed manager at New Orleans, and he later became vice-president of the company. In this position he served with credit until his retirement in 1939. As a matter of fact, he distinguished himself in the great work of establishing good will between the people of the United States and Latin America, and also in promoting sanitation throughout the Middle American countries in an effort to stamp out the diseases which harassed the inhabitants. In this worthwhile endeavor, which succeeded admirably, he formed a close friendship with the presidents of the different nations of Central and South America, and won the admiration of the people, who were unstinting in their cooperation. As early as 1905 he had fitted out a ship for the purpose of carrying with him many of the most eminent doctors of America to visit all the Middle American ports at which the United Fruit Company held stations for trading. He will long be remembered by the people in whose welfare he took so great an interest. At the same time he did a very worthwhile service for his company, which has many thousands of men and women employed in and about the ports of Middle America.

The United Fruit Company is more than an institution set up for the purpose of making money for the stockholders who own it and the men who operate it. It is also a great factor in the advancement of American civilization. It is a tremendously rich organization, which has under its control approximately 500,000 acres of improved land and land under cultivation, and it operates more than 60 excellent cargo and passenger vessels, and more than 4,400 miles of railroad. In these vast projects more than 70,000 persons are employed; the greater part of them (about 90 percent) are stationed in Middle America. For these employees and their children the company has built thirteen up-to-date hospitals throughout the tropics, and has provided also many field dispensaries for the promotion of good health among the workers. In one section of Cuba these health services have reduced malaria cases from 50 percent among the employees (which was a common average) to 1 percent in recent years. Certainly this is an excellent showing.

In order that the children of the workers stationed in the tropics may have the same advantages as those in the States, the company has provided free schools where the groups are large enough to justify it, and is somewhat ahead of the States in furnishing also special diet programs designed to build resistance to disease and to promote health and strength generally. As a matter of fact, the medical staff of the United Fruit Company has made a remarkable achievement in stamping out or controlling many tropical diseases, and the result has been as much for the benefit of the natives of that country as for the employees of the company. This excellent work for the good of many people, who would have been unable to do it for themselves, meant an advantage to the company also, for workers healthy and strong obviously can do a better job. But it is a fine example of the advantage of capitalism over communism, which, with wealth centralized and controlled by the government, would have no special interest in the welfare of any particular group. What the United Fruit Company did for the benefit of its workers gave comfort also to the people of the surrounding country, and the scientific discoveries made by its medical staff were freely given to the world to be used for the general good of humanity. Without a large amount of capital and facilities for employing it placed in the hands of a few liberal and honorable men, who had the intelligence to recognize their responsibility, nothing constructive could have been done, and those sections of Middle America which have been made habitable and healthful would still be infested with the same diseases and inconveniences which for centuries kept them from progressing. There are large corporations with great capital structures not so far advanced as the United Fruit Company in what may be termed their human relations, but they will in time benefit by the experience of others or they will not long survive, for the attitude of the captains of industry toward the welfare of their employees and the community in general will be a strong factor in the future.

Some years ago the United Fruit Company decided, quite naturally, to increase the consumption of bananas in the United States, for production was running somewhat ahead of the demand. But the management of the company wisely concluded that before launching an advertising campaign it would be well to find out why the American people should eat more bananas. In those days the rice millers were extolling the virtues of rice—it mixed well with other foods, and was cheap. The orange-growers were recommending the orange as the health fruit; and the salmon-packers were acquainting the public with the value of that fish in the American diet. Was there any good reason for asking the people to eat more bananas? The United Fruit Company would find out. Enlisting the cooperation of eminent doctors in various parts of the country, its medical staff found that the banana has a high nutritive value, and that it is remarkably easy to digest. They found also that it contains appreciable quantities of mineral salts, such as phosphates, sulphates, chlorides of potassium, sodium, magnesium, calcium, and a fair amount of iron. Two leading pediatricians at New Orleans, Dr. Edwin A. Socola and Dr. Marx D. Sterbcow, made exhaustive experiments in feeding bananas to infants. They found bananas to be the only food that some sick babies could digest, and that infants with diarrhea recovered on a diet of ripe bananas. Cases of malnutrition also were cured by a temporary diet of ripe bananas, and the patients were brought back to normal health.

When these facts were found they were given to the public in a big way, and not only the United Fruit Company but all the banana growers of Middle America, and the fruit dealers as well as the people of North America were benefited accordingly.

But to return to the river front of New Orleans, where the United Fruit Company unloads about 6,000,000 bunches of bananas a year, the Dock Board has granted preferential of approximately half a mile wharf space to the company to be used exclusively for loading and unloading its bananas and for handling its passengers and its general cargo, which consists chiefly of foodstuffs, building materials, and manufactured products. In 1953 about 194 cargo and passenger vessels of the United Fruit Company's fleet entered and cleared at New Orleans. From the cargoes which arrive here shipments are made to various states via railroad and barge transportation. Many passengers which come on these ships travel by train and plane to the cities of the West or the Middle West.

It was estimated in 1955 by Freddie Maher, general passenger agent for the United Fruit Company, that the ships of his company arriving and clearing at this port carried more than a thousand passengers a month. Mr. Maher remembers when the company's ships were small and carried only a few passengers, but as trade and traffic between the tropics and New Orleans increased, larger ships were built and put into service. The average ship now carries as many as a hundred passengers, and provides comfortable quarters for them.

These 194 ship-calls provide work for the New Orleans river front labor, for trucking companies, warehouses, and for many other firms. In its Southern Domestic Division, the company has 350 regular employees stationed at its office, located in the United Fruit Building, and many hundreds of workers are employed on the river front.

What the United Fruit Company has done in the way of developing banana-growing and other industries in Middle America has been of inestimable value to New Orleans, for during the past half century it has opened up trade channels not only for its own products, but has supplied the facilities, such as transportation, both water and rail, for others to develop industries and trade. Moreover, acting as a good-will agent, it has brought about a better understanding between North Americans and Latin Americans, who, speaking a different language and living according to different customs, were strangers in business and in their social life, although they did not, as the crow flies, live far apart. Thus, the United Fruit Company is essentially a part of the history of the river front and the city of New Orleans itself.

For more than twenty years the United Fruit Company was the only enterprise of any consequence supplying bananas to the New Orleans market. There were some individuals with small fleets of schooners in the trade, and they were in the main unsuccessful. But around 1896 there came forth four able citizens of New Orleans who were, from a small beginning, to build a banana importing enterprise which eventually became a formidable competitor of the United Fruit Company. Three of these men were brothers: Joseph, Felix, and Luca Vaccaro; the other, Salvador D'Antoni, was a brother-in-law of one of the Vaccaros. They were in the retail banana business, which had been profitable, and they bought a schooner which a bankrupt importer had for sale, and organized an importing business known as Vaccaro Brothers and Company, for the purpose of importing bananas and other fruit from the tropics. This name was later changed to The Standard Fruit and Steamship Company, which built and operated a fleet of steamships known as the Vaccaro Line. The Standard Fruit and Steamship Company, with large plantations in Central America, and magnificent steamships, traveling to nearly all ports in the world, is one of the largest of American industries.

Antique Furniture in Louisiana Before 1860

Royal Street in New Orleans in 1834 was the locality of more than one hundred furniture-manufacturing establishments, according to a historical record published in that year. Before and after that time, furniture craftsmen carried on their businesses in or near Royal Street. Mallard, Siebrecht, Seignouret — these are some of the well-known cabinet-makers of the early nineteenth century who were established in New Orleans.

An advertisement appearing in 1852 reads:

FANCY FURNISHING WAREHOUSE, 67 Royal and 80 Bienville Streets. P. Mallard & Co., importers of French Carved Rosewood and Mahogany Furniture. Looking-glasses, Sevres China and Porcelain Ware; Clocks, Crystal, Bohemian Glass, Porcelain and Bronze Mantel Ornaments, etc.

Foreign Influence on Louisiana Furniture

The first colonial furniture was of the plainest sort, having been built hurriedly to supply actual needs, and was usually made of cypress. Later, however, more luxurious furniture was imported from France. During the early period of French domination, there were not many cabinet-makers in Louisiana, as the rich planters could well afford to import furniture from France. There were, nevertheless, some imitations of imported furniture manufactured here at that time. It is very seldom at present that one discovers an example of an imported piece from that period. Since then there have been three fires, and the Civil War. The destruction of the war, as well as the economic situation following it, resulted in the scattering and loss of this early furniture.

In "Good Furniture Magazine" of June, 1926, Amelia Leavitt Hill outlines early Louisiana history and shows its influence on furniture. The first governor of Louisiana was appointed in 1689. New Orleans was founded in 1718 and became the capital of the colony in 1722. The territory was ceded to Spain by France in 1762 and was returned in 1800. The Louisiana Purchase took place in 1803. The period of French domination lasted fifty years; of Spanish domination, thirty-eight years; followed by a brief period of French authority before the country became a part of the United States. Therefore foreign influence reached Louisiana via France and Spain. During the Spanish régime, French influence continued to be strongly felt.

Louisiana Climate Influenced Furniture Styles

The dampness of the Louisiana climate influenced furnishing conditions, and was responsible for the use of the ball-shaped brass feet, since wooden feet were susceptible to climatic conditions. This is also why marble was found on tops of tables and bureaus. Since dampness affects veneer, woods not requiring veneer to appear at their best were popular — rosewood, for instance. Mahogany was used too, even though it requires veneer; but other woods peculiar to this section were more popular.

The warmth of the climate made large rooms a necessity. Rooms were usually twenty to twenty-five feet square and fourteen to eighteen feet high. Massive furniture was needed to fill them. Beds of the period are especially illustrative of large-scale furniture. It may be an exaggeration to say that such beds might accommodate from five to six persons. Four posts were used on the beds to provide for the mosquito bar.

Armoires also were large and massive, because of the enormous rooms which had no closets. Again due to the climate, hinges were not generally used on these armoires, or "armors," but instead there were pivots at the top and bottom on which the doors could swing.

Spanish Influence

The chief Spanish contribution to furniture was the Bautac chair, in which leather was firmly stretched over a plain wooden frame. There were no arms, but merely a curving of the frame, and almost C-shaped seat. Later the English influence led to the Bautac chair's being provided with arms, and sometimes with wings. These chairs were light, comfortable, and picturesque.

Simeon Seignouret, Cabinet-Maker

The first great New Orleans cabinet-maker was Siméon Seignouret. He specialized in bed-room and dining-room furniture, and preferred to work in rosewood and mahogany. His designs were delicate even in heavy articles of furniture. The carving was always cut from the body of the furniture itself. It is said that his initial "S" was in some form or other worked into the decoration of every one of his finished pieces. This story arose probably from the frequency of his use of scroll and curves, and his habit of breaking panels with delicate S-like motifs. Delicate rippling beading is also characteristic of Seignouret.

P. Mallard (1838 to 1860)

Mallard succeeded Seignouret, and worked from 1838 to 1860. He was born in Sèvres, France, in 1809. He completed his studies in Paris and arrived in New Orleans in his twenties and opened a shop at 55 Royal Street, according to G. William Knott in "The Antiquarian". "By 1838," says Mr. Knott, "the establishment, consisting of many skilled workmen, had grown to considerable proportions."

Mallard used Seignouret's designs, but combined them with original motifs. He liked to work in mahogany and rosewood, and used linings of bird's-eye maple. In place of Seignouret's rippling, he used a design suggestive of egg and dart. His beds are particularly distinctive. They have a canopy, as well as four posts, supported from the back and covering two-thirds of the bed itself. The canopy was generally lined with silk or satin. Tufted satin was popular, though not sanitary.

Mallard's armoires were very large, but his bureaus were smaller, and on a more attractive scale for modern use. His chairs, though not conspicuous for fine carving, are light and delicate.

Mallard's name appears in the city directory as cabinet-maker, upholsterer, and furniture dealer.

John H. Belter, Northern Cabinet-Maker

John H. Belter, a New York cabinet-maker, was popular in Louisiana from 1844 to 1848. His furniture was notable for the extraordinary elaboration of its carving, which was like wooden lace-work, about six inches deep. Rosewood was popular with him. Aside from his elaborate carving, the most striking characteristic of his pieces is their shape. Backs of sofas and chairs were deeply curved.

In spite of the fact that Belter used much glue in his furniture, which made it unsuited to a damp climate, its undisputed fine quality accounts for its popularity in Louisiana.

The "Dark Ages"

After Mallard, the dark ages of American interior decoration, South as well as North, approached, according to Amelia Hill in her survey in "Good Furniture." But before the storm of black walnut broke, labor difficulties, arising after the Civil War, forced the New Orleans furniture manufacturers to move to Cincinnati, where they produced a kind of furniture which was labelled by unknowing people as "Colonial." Largely in rosewood, these pieces consist of ugly imitations of Louis XVI types, full of meaningless curves and ungraceful lines. They were cheap in construction and workmanship, but apparently because of their French suggestion, they found a ready market in Louisiana.

With the manufacture of this "Colonial" furniture, the period of inferior production set in. The days of the charming work of Seignouret and Mallard had passed.

Louis XVI furniture is the earliest furniture still to be found in New Orleans in any considerable amount.

The Medical History of New Orleans
New Orleans Hospitals

From the beginning of the Crescent City's history, colonists had hospitals and, as critics are wont to do, people complained about the service. Dr. Pierre Manadé, a protegé of Bienville, directed the New Orleans Hospital in 1723, and was criticized by Jacques de la Chaise, the Company of the Indies director, for failure to provide adequate medicines and aid to the patients. De la Chaise felt that the Gray Sisters of the Order of St. Vincent de Paul would do a better job and, as a result, "the sick would have more assistance from these sisters than they have from infirmarians who steal their rations."

The following year, 1724, a dispute broke out between Paul Perry, the company-appointed director of the hospital, and Dr. Alexandre Viel, the surgeon-major of the hospital. Dr. Viel, a noted botanist and surgeon and corresponding member of the French Royal Academy of Science, had complained about lack of medicines and financial aid, but Perry claimed that these were flimsy excuses designed to cover up Dr. Viel's true reasons for failure to provide adequate medical aid to two small-pox victims: lack of recognition for his contributions to the colony.

In an effort to remedy the poor care and wasteful administration of the New Orleans hospital, the Jesuit superiors, in cooperation with the company directors, sought to bring from France a number of Ursuline nuns to minister to the educational and medical needs of the nascent colony. In 1726 it was agreed that a charity hospital be established for New Orleans which would receive the poor gratis and accept paying patients who were able to pay their own fees. The company agreed to subsidize the hospital until a plantation donated to the Ursulines could produce enough profits to support the hospital without the subsidy.

The New Orleans charity hospital was often referred to as the Jean Louis Hospital for the Poor after the French sailor who had donated funds for that purpose during the time of Bienville. Many years later the New Orleans creoles hotly protested against the usurpation of their traditional control over the charity hospital. On December 13, 1782, Mario de Reggio reported to the New Orleans Cabildo (municipal council) that a charity hospital had existed in the town from the very beginning and was supported by the alms, legacies and bequests of the philanthropic colonists. Every three years the leading residents met together and examined the accounts of the hospital. As it grew and expanded, they named an administrator and treasurer to take care of these duties, subject to periodic examination by the settlers in cooperation with the parish priest.

Reggio's report failed to note that the Ursulines had labored under many handicaps with never sufficient money to provide necessary medical aid for the New Orleans poor. There were too few sheets, mosquito bars, basins, gauze, syringes, rations or medicines for the needy patients, particularly after the Natchez Massacre of 1729 when refugees and orphans poured into New Orleans requiring medical aid. This virtually drained the pharmacy of medicines, the larders of food, and forced too many people into the already cramped rooms.

The Ursulines planned for the future with amazing optimism, however, and in the school they operated for forty day students and twenty-four boarding pupils — all girls — they hoped to find future nurses and hospital administrators. The Ursulines had one other problem to face: the hospital was located in a temporary shelter at one end of town, while the convent was at the other extremity, forcing the nuns to violate cloister rules by parading through the streets of New Orleans to minister to the sick.

Spanish occupation of New Orleans on an effective basis took place in 1769, but the problems faced by the hospital of charity continued to plague the colonial administrators. The Jean Louis Charity Hospital was seriously damaged by hurricanes during the years 1779, 1780 and 1781, and the Spanish government sought to rebuild the hospital by using the materials from the old one. This and the fact that a new administrator was appointed by Governor-general Bernardo de Gálvez and his successor, Esteban Miró, provoked the leading creoles to protest against usurpation of their traditional rights, but Gálvez stoutly claimed that the government alone had exclusive right over the hospital.

It was a Spaniard named Andrés Almonester y Roxas (1725-1798) who came to the city's aid on more than one occasion regarding its medical needs. On May 1, 1784, he petitioned the New Orleans Cabildo for permission to donate from his own pocket the necessary funds with which to rebuild the charity hospital provided that he, as sponsor, be allowed, under Spanish laws, the right to name the hospital personnel. The Cabildo agreed, and the first patient was admitted to the new brick-and-lime structure on October 1, 1786. The hospital was then valued at $114,000.

Dedicated to San Carlos, the patron saint of the Spanish King Charles III, the St. Charles Charity Hospital has continued its existence to the present day. The chapel of the hospital was dedicated to the Advocation of the Virgin of Con-

CHARITY HOSPITAL, New Orleans, April 16, 1859. From Ballou's Pictorial Drawing-room Companion.

solation and each of the four wards was dedicated respectively to Sts. Joseph, Matthew, Bernard and James.

Almonester provided the hospital with twenty-four beds, linens, clothing, food, the services of several Negro servants and an annual subsidy of $1,500. It is said that the disastrous fire of 1788, which did over two million dollars damage, also ravaged the hospital, but this is not certain because Almonester reported that he admitted seventy patients to the hospital at that time. Almonester was not always so charitable, however, and in 1787 he told a patient named Pedro Roger to either pay fifteen dollars a day or face immediate dismissal.

Under a 1591 Spanish law, all persons who founded hospitals and endowed them with their own funds were entitled to the patronage power in those hospitals, which meant they could appoint the personnel. From 1786 until 1792 Almonester exercised this power, but on May 1, 1792, Governor-general Carondelet usurped Almonester's powers and appointed the Louisiana treasurer, Gilberto Leonard, as hospital administrator until a Spanish decree of 1793 restored Almonester's powers. It is ironic to note that during the period from 1792 to 1794 when Almonester was deprived from his patronage power, the Cabildo appealed to him for more funds. The benefactor hotly replied that he had already done much for the hospital and probably would continue to do so on a voluntary basis, but he deplored the appointment of a surgeon without his approval. Almonester donated $500 to the hospital in his 1794 will.

When Major Amos Stoddard of the American occupation forces came to New Orleans in 1803 he praised the "honorable monument to the memory of its founder" and pointed out that

"Poor Spanish subjects, and sometimes strangers, (provided they paid half a dollar per day) were admitted into this asylum. Those entirely destitute were admitted gratis. They had medicine, sustenance, and other aid, afforded them," he wrote.

There were other hospitals in New Orleans in addition to the St. Charles Charity Hospital. In 1802 an American hospital was established at New Orleans with funds from the United States Congress and administered by the American consul in the city. Spanish regulations of 1776 dictated the rules for good order and sound medical aid for its royal hospitals, one of which was established at New Orleans primarily to care for military and civilian employees there. In 1781 the Spanish government provided $23,412 in subsidies for the royal hospital with a staff composed of a physician earning $600 a year; a surgeon-major with the same salary; a chief medic at $360; additional personnel, food, medicines and utensils. By 1791 salaries alone amounted to $5,148 for the auditor, superintendent, commissioner for entries, physician-major, chief surgeon, chaplain, apothecary, chief medic, three medics, two orderlies, an assistant apothecary, a cook and a male nurse.

After several cases of leprosy were reported in 1785, Andrés Almonester y Roxas came to the city's aid once again by providing a special four-room hospital located on Almonester's plantation adjacent to that of Joseph Cultia near what was to become the Carondelet Canal leading to Lake Pontchartrain from the city. It was called, appropriately, the San Lázaro Hospital, in memory of the leprous beggar Lazarus, whom Jesus cured. Segregated facilities were provided for white and black. At first Almonester offered $2,100 a year as subsidy, the money coming from his property rentals near the Plaza de Armas (Jackson Square) but the hospital administrator, Luis Toutant Beauregard (uncle of Louisiana's Napoleon-in-Gray, Pierre Gustave Toutant Beauregard), was hard pressed to keep the hospital on an even financial keel and, at one time patients were forced to subsist on less than seven cents a day! When Beauregard died and the hospital was threatened with no funds at all while his estate was being settled, the city provided adequate funds on an interim basis.

Five lepers ultimately died from the disease, but in 1785 the discovery of no new cases led to optimism. The Spanish authorities recognized the necessity of quarantine action, and it refused a petition from Francisco Roquigny in 1785 that his son be released from the leper house because Dr. Esteban Foignet de Pellegrue had testified he had been cured. It seems that other physicians who examined the youth were not in agreement and they recommended that he be kept in the hospital until thoroughly cured of the disease. At the same time, the Cabildo asked that Nicolás Forstall, a councilman who had charge of the lepers, provide the hospital with two steers for their nourishment.

From time to time, as necessity dictated, emergency quarantine hospitals were established. In 1779 when the outbreak of small-pox threatened to become epidemic, Governor-general Gálvez called together seventy leading citizens and told them that the royal treasury would be used to transport all victims of the disease to the other side of the river where they would be lodged and cared for by a physician appointed for the purpose. A royal decree of September 4, 1785, governed quarantines and the treatment of small-pox, and this regulation was duly entered in the Cabildo records of March 8, 1786, for the guidance of the city fathers.

Francisco Gil, surgeon of the Monastery of San Lorenzo in Spain, had written a volume warmly applauded by the Madrid Academy of Medicine. Entitled **Curacion de viruelas y formas de evitar su contraccion,** the volume formed part of the New Orleans Cabildo library and was consulted on matters affecting "the cure of small-pox and means of avoiding its contagion." When a boat-load of Negro slaves arriving in New Orleans in 1787 was found to have several of the unfortunate wretches suffering from the disease, the Cabildo recalled Article 65 of Gil's book and took over the house and lot being rented by Carlos Lajonchere Daunoy, located opposite New Orleans on the other side of the Mississippi. Here they located a hospital and quarantined those suffering from small-pox.

In 1788 the city fathers recognized the connection between disease and the problem of burying too many cadavers in the New Orleans cemeteries, and they decided there was a danger to public health in such practices. In 1799 the government and physicians met to consider ways of improving public health in New Orleans, and one of their suggestions, in keeping with the atmospheric theory of disease prevalent in colonial Louisiana, was to drain the swamps and provide adequate sewage control.

In 1800 the schooner **Theodora** bound for New Orleans from Baltimore, was halted at the Spanish post of San Phelipe de Placaminas, below New Orleans. Dr. Juan Malard, the surgeon of the post, reported that two crewmen were stricken with small-pox, one having broken out with the disease a month earlier and the other only a week prior to their arrival. Dr. Malard recommended that the ship be placed in quarantine immediately.

Eleven days later, on June 22, 1800, Captain Samuel Hopkins of the schooner petitioned for release from quarantine as follows:

"We the undersigned do certify, that we have used all the means in our power to eradicate every particle of the disease for which we are here quarantined, that the man who had it last, has been twenty-two days well, and able to do his duty, that his woolen clothes were thrown overboard before we entered the mouth of the Mississippi, and that since we have been at Plachaminas (sic), the vessel has been washed night and morning with vinegar, and all the woolen clothes on board, washed, aired, and sprinkled with vinegar. From the precautions thus made use of, and the well known nature of the disease, we believe we are entirely free from all contagious matter."

The ship's surgeon, Dr. John Mackey, concurred with the belief that the disease was arrested and that there "is neither risk nor impropriety in permitting the vessel to proceed to New Orleans." The vessel was finally allowed to proceed on course, but it is readily apparent that a zealous Spanish government, in cooperation with skilled physicians and surgeons, tried to protect the people of the Crescent City from illness as best they could.

All medical personnel in New Orleans and Louisiana were required to obtain a license from the Spanish government. One of the first to receive such permission was Dr. Francisco Guischar, a graduate surgeon from Havana, who received in 1767 from Governor Antonio de Ulloa license to practice in New Orleans. "He is a person of skill in his profession," wrote Ulloa, "especially in cases of difficult childbirth and sickness of the face and mouth, as he has already proved by his notable work." Dr. Guischar's medical books, instruments and medicines were admitted duty-free to the city.

Surgeons such as Dr. Pedro Bellora and Pedro Gallegos were in New Orleans briefly in 1768 and 1778 respectively, but they obtained permission to return to Havana after a brief stay. Dr. Thomas Canales y Roquer, who had been appointed surgeon for the third battalion of the Louisiana Infantry Regiment, asked permission to return to Spain.

One of the earliest examples of licensing occurred in the case of Jean Peyroux de Rochemolive who petitioned the New Orleans Cabildo for permission to practice pharmacy in New Orleans. Dr. Lebeau, the royal physician of New Orleans under the French, examined Peyroux and concluded that his long training and experience entitled him to a license to practice, and it was issued on January 12, 1770, with the following stipulations:

1) He must maintain accurate records in a register with the name and signature of persons obtaining prescriptions in order to prevent unauthorized persons from obtaining drugs.

2) No prescription would be dispensed without prior permission of the government.

3) Prices for all medicines would be arranged in a posted and government-approved tariff.

4) No alterations in prescriptions would be made by the apothecary.

5) Until Spanish procedures might be established, the customs of Paris would prevail.

6) No poisonous drugs would be administered without special permission from government.

Spanish surgeons and physicians who worked for the government were hardly over-paid, even by contemporary standards. Head surgeons and physicians at the royal hospitals earned an average of $600 a year, while the **practicante-mayor**, or chief medic, earned but $360 annually. Still, there were fringe benefits to government service. A retirement fund called the **Monte Pio** enabled surgeons to contribute eight percent of their income to a pension fund. Unfortunately, there were also taxes. Following appointment, one-half of the first year's salary plus 18% transportation charges was deducted in the traditional **media annata** tax.

Physicians of the Spanish Period

It is impossible to determine how many physicians, surgeons, pharmacists, hospital administrators, medics, and other medical personnel served at New Orleans during the Spanish period, but the following include most of those who applied for their licenses or who are listed in the payroll accounts for the Spanish colony. For convenient reference, the names have been alphabetized.

Alliot, Paul. French surgeon expelled from New Orleans for practicing without a license in 1803, although he claimed it was because of the professional jealousy of Dr. Joseph Montegut.

Champignon, Luis. Manager of the hospital on Toulouse Street in 1791.

Cherme, Phelipe. Petitioned to be admitted to practice as surgeon on June 10, 1785.

Cornaud, Joseph. Petitioned for license to practice as surgeon on February 12, 1790. Admitted to practice. Examined bleeding piles of André David at Natchitoches and recommended treatment on August 1, 1794.

Couturier, Pedro. Physician on Toulouse Street, 1791.

Cruzat de San Marcial, Juan. Physician asking permission to practice in New Orleans on October 24, 1794. Examination conducted by Drs. Estevan Foignet de Pellegrue and Robert Dow.

Donal(d)son, Robert. Petitioned for license to practice as surgeon in New Orleans on November 25, 1785.

Dow, Robert, Scottish physician who began practice in New Orleans in 1778. Treated leprosy. Lived on Royal Street, 1791. Outstanding physician of New Orleans for four decades. Gayarré describes him as "full of genial, exhuberant kindness for all his fellow human beings, of a florid complexion, of convivial habits . . . a great authority, and no member of his profession ever acquired more popularity." Founder of the College of Orleans and president of the first New Orleans Medical Society in 1822. Close friend of Dr. Benjamin Rush, with whom he breakfasted in Philadelphia in 1800.

Dunoyer, Luis. Petitioned for license to practice as surgeon. Examined by Drs. Montegut and Santiago Hurzolle and admitted to practice on August 27, 1779.

Escoffie, Carlos. Asked permission to practice as surgeon on November 19, 1790. Examined by Drs. Santiago Leduc and Pedro Couturier and was admitted to practice on May 20, 1791. Listed as an apothecary living on Royal Street, November 6, 1791.

Faure, Luis. Physician and surgeon-major of the Spanish Mississippi Squadron, he was born in Rochelle, France in 1763. He obtained a license to practice as surgeon in Louisiana from Governor-general Miró on October 14, 1784. He served at the royal hospitals of Natchez, Baton Rouge, Nogales, and San Fernando de las Barrancas.

Fernandez, Jose. Surgeon living on St. Philip Street in 1791. Served as surgeon for the battalion staffing the Mississippi Squadron from October 30 until December 4, 1794, when replaced by Dr. Faure.

Fernandez, Jose Maria. Mulatto native of Havana who served as bleeder on the schooner **La Fina** at $15 a month in 1794. Sentenced to serve on the public works of New Orleans for one year in New Orleans. Served with the crew of the galley **La Leal** in 1795. Fulfilled posts of bleeder and surgeon with skill and admirable support from his fellow crewmen.

Fleitas, Domingo. Born in 1750, he served as medic-in-chief during the Gálvez expedition against Forts Bute de Manchak and Baton Rouge in 1779. He served as surgeon major on the Spanish brigantine **Galveztown** from June 14, 1780, following the shipwreck of the **Santa Catalina,** alias **La Ventura,** off Mobile Point in 1780, during which tragedy he lost all his professional papers and titles. As medic-in-chief of the New Orleans royal hospital from September 1, 1783, he petitioned on May 18, 1792, for permission to practice surgery and presented seven documents from persons qualified to report on his experience. They show he was a surgeon for the Canary

Island colonists who came to Louisiana in 1778 and settled near New Iberia. From June 14, 1792, he also served as surgeon for the New Orleans militia, and later as apothecary for the Royal Hospital of New Orleans. On May 25, 1792, he passed the examination for surgeon given by Drs. Pellegrue, Montegut and Leduc.

Fortin, Luis. Asked license to practice as surgeon on September 14, 1792. Examined by Drs. Pellegrue, Montegut and Leduc and passed. Became surgeon of the Plaquemines post at $360 a year from 1793 until January 1, 1796.

Fougnet de Pellegrue, Estevan. Royal physician of the New Orleans hospital with salary of $600 annually. Born in 1746, he came to Louisiana on May 14, 1785 with charge of the Acadian families. He was a warm supporter of Governor Bernardo de Gálvez. In the fire of 1788 he lost his entire stock of drugs, utensils and furniture valued at more than $6,000. He frequently examined military personnel at the royal hospital in New Orleans to determine whether they were fit for duty. He lived on Bourbon Street in 1791 but owned a lot and homes on Conde Street which he rented out to serve as barracks for the Picket of Dragoons of Louisiana in 1799 and 1800. He was married.

Gil, Andres. Served during 1786 and 1787 as apothecary aide at the New Orleans Royal Hospital. Also served at Natchez, Nogales, Baton Rouge, and Pensacola. His pay at New Orleans was only $8 a month plus rations, and he asked for a raise to feed his wife and children.

Gonzalez, Juan. Medic of the New Orleans Royal Hospital. Was born in 1761. Became a medic on March 1, 1779 and served in the Gálvez expeditions of 1779 and against Pensacola in 1781. Gálvez named him medic second-class in 1779 at a salary of $15 a month. In 1793 he was only earning $192 a year as medic, although he was married and had served almost 15 years. On December 12, 1793, he petitioned the government against the estate of Father Francisco de Caldas for the sum of $12 for bleedings and treatment of a tumor on the late priest's Negress slave Rosa.

Hurzolle, Santiago. Surgeon of New Orleans who examined the qualifications of Dr. Luis Dunoyer as surgeon on August 27, 1779.

Labie, Jose. Surgeon of New Orleans who lost over $6,000 in the fire of March 21, 1788. On November 6, 1791, he lived on Conti Street. He served in 1792 as surgeon of the first battalion of the Louisiana Infantry Regiment, and in 1800 served with the expedition sent to recapture the post of San Marcos de Apalache (St. Marks, Florida) from William Augustus Bowles.

Lebeau, Dr. Royal physician of New Orleans who examined Jean Peyroux de Rochemolive for pharmacy license on March 12, 1769.

LeDuc, Santiago. Surgeon of the New Orleans Charity Hospital in 1792, although he had been in New Orleans at least as early as September 8, 1783, when he witnessed the last will of Antonio Crespo y Neve. In 1791 examined Dr. Carlos Escoufier for a surgeon's license. In 1802 he is listed as "surgeon of number" for New Orleans when he sued the estate of Francisco Barras for $17.50 in past-due bills for medicines, care and house visits. The suit was not contested.

Loubie, Carlos. Pharmacist and chemist of New Orleans and member of the Royal Pharmacy College of Havana. Examined at New Orleans by Gabriel Peyroux de Rochemolive on February 11, 1785, and admitted to practice under regulations established by O'Reilly. Was imprisoned for uttering seditious remarks in 1793 by Governor-general Carondelet and then sent for 26 months exile to Havana, after which he returned to testify at the trial of Carondelet's term of office in 1797.

Misas, Juan de. A soldier of the Louisiana Infantry Regiment who served as medic at the post of San Phelipe de Placaminas in 1799-1800, then went to New Orleans, but returned to his earlier post in 1801 and remained until discharge on September 1, 1802.

Montegut, Joseph. One of the outstanding surgeons and physicians of the colonial period, he was born in 1739, a descendant of Norman ancestors who invaded Italy in the eighth and ninth centuries. Dr. Montegut came to Louisiana about 1760 and was married to Françoise de Lisle Dupart, a native of the colony. Within a few years he became the first resident physician of the New Orleans hospital and served without pay. He inspected the local jail and ministered to the needs of the inmates and checked incoming ships to insure the crews were free from disease. He served with Gálvez in the Fort Bute de Manchak and Baton Rouge campaigns of 1779 and the Mobile campaign of 1780. In 1781 he was named surgeon of the First Battalion of the Louisiana Infantry Regiment, and on August 1, 1781, named surgeon-major of the royal hospital at an annual salary of $600. Here he performed routine surgery, inspected military personnel to determine their fitness for duty, examined the qualifications of physicians and surgeons requesting permission to practice medicine in Louisiana, inspected cadets of the Louisiana Infantry Regiment, and made daily visits to the hospital. He was threatened in 1795 by a patient named Corporal Gabriel González who brandished a razor to prevent anyone approaching him. Dr. Montegut testified in court cases where medical knowledge was a factor. He also maintained an important private practice which included some of the wealthiest and most prominent patients in the colony such as the philanthropist Andrés Almonester y Roxas and the governor-general, the Baron de Carondelet. Governor William C. C. Claiborne appointed him as a member of the first Board of Health for New Orleans in 1804 when the Americans took over Louisiana, and the following year he helped organize the College of Orleans and served on its board of regents. In 1811, in company with other surgeons and physicians, he urged the draining of stagnant pools and the cleaning up of the city in an effort to improve public health. He was named to the council of administration for the St. Charles Charity Hospital on November 13, 1811, but in 1817, when he was asked to join one of the newly-organized medical societies, he tendered his regrets, explaining that the "infirmities of age and his love of solitude" made him decline. As late as 1814 he was still characterized as extremely pro-Spanish along with his sons, one of whom was registrar of births and death for Orleans Parish in 1811.

Morain, Jean. A native of San Malo, Brittany (France), he was born in 1736, the son of Francisco Marin and Francisca Biesie Marin. He learned medicine at San Malo and at Cap Française in the Caribbean, having studied at the latter city under the royal physician Dr. Baradas. He was admitted to practice surgery in New Orleans on July 27, 1781.

Morel, Esteban Henriquez. In 1777, when he arrived at New Orleans, it was said that there was no physician in the city at that time and, although a foreigner, he was immediately admitted to practice.

Ocon, Josef. Chief pharmacist of the Royal Hospital of New Orleans. Born in 1743, he was named pharmacist second-class for the expedition being formed against Mobile in 1779 and, following the capture of that British post in 1780, on April 30, 1780, he was named chief pharmacist of the New Orleans hospital, taking charge in November of that year of the duties of majordomo, commissioner of entries, quartermaster and orderly, and serving until July 31, 1781, without pay. His superiors lauded his good aptitude, talent, conduct and application. On November 6, 1791, he lived on St. Philip Street; he was married.

Paulus, Peter (Pedro). On November 20, 1789, he delivered his petition to the New Orleans Cabildo accompanied by testimonials from several citizens of the town who had been cured of venereal disease by his methods. He asked to treat such diseases and, after examining the documents, the council approved unanimously to allow him to treat only venereal diseases, but nothing else not having direct connection with the disease. On November 6, 1791, he lived on Ursuline Street and was known as a surgeon. He was a Pennsylvania Dutch colonizer with a plan for populating Louisiana, but was not too careful with his finances: in 1797 he was sued by a free Negress named Gabriela to collect a past-due obligation.

Peyroux de Rochemolive, Gabriel. Apothecary living on Dumaine Street, November 6, 1791.

Peyroux de Rochemolive, Jean. Petitioned on March 12, 1769, to practice pharmacy in New Orleans. Approved by Cabildo on January 12, 1770, in action which established procedures for pharmacists.

Pfeiffer, George. Admitted to practice surgery and serve as physician at New Orleans on January 22, 1800.

Robin, Lamberto. After examination by Drs. Pellegrue, Montegut, and Commissioners Almonester and Ducros, he was admitted as surgeon on September 28, 1792.

Rouelle, Juan Carlos. Physician trained at the University of Rains (Reims?), he was admitted to practice in New Orleans on March 27, 1778. For the sum of $50 he volunteered to go to Natchitoches during an epidemic in May, 1778, discover the cause and check it.

Salva, Federico. An apothecary who lived on Royal Street on November 6, 1791.

Senac, Francisco. After examination by Drs. Dow, Montegut, Couturier and LeDuc, he was admitted to practice surgery in New Orleans on June 20, 1783. He was probably known as Juan Senac also, for a surgeon by that name treated a Negress who was gravely wounded in the arm, necessitating an amputation performed by Dr. Senac. He was not paid his fee of $55, and he was forced to sue Luis Toutant Beauregard, the owner of the slave, who then asked to reimbursement from the Runaway Slave Fund. This occurred in 1790.

Sougrin, Antonio Francisco. Surgeon examined to practice in New Orleans by Drs. Dow, Montegut, Labie, and Leduc on June 6, 1783.

Traver, Marcos Antonio. Surgeon-general of the Regiment of Spain who left the expedition which conquered Pensacola in 1781 and returned to New Orleans where he remained only a few months before returning to Havana on December 20, 1781.

Vaucheret, Enrique. Medic of the Royal Hospital of New Orleans at an annual salary of $180, he was a young bachelor of 19 when he was appointed on September 1, 1792.

Vietrao, Diego. Licensed as a surgeon for New Orleans and Louisiana after examination and approved by Cabildo on August 12, 1785.

Vigne, Josef Santiago. Requested examination for license to practice surgery in New Orleans on July 9, 1784.

Villamil, Pedro. Manager of the hospital on St. Philip Street as of November 6, 1791.

Vincente, Santiago. French surgeon, educated at Montpellier, where he received his degree February 20, 1756. Accepted to practice at Madrid on October 14, 1765. Served in the naval squadrons. On December 12, 1777, he was admitted to practice surgery in New Orleans following his oath of loyalty to the Spanish sovereign. He requested a government intervention to collect a debt owed by a Mr. Boume of Upper Louisiana in 1797.

Viure, Jacinto. Army medic who served in the expedition to Pensacola and stayed briefly at New Orleans until December, 1781, when he returned to Havana.

Zerban, Federico. Apothecary of New Orleans who asked to be examined by fellow-pharmacists Ocon and Peyroux de Rochemolive on March 2, 1792.

REFERENCES — PHYSICIANS OF THE SPANISH PERIOD

NOTE: Most of the information was gleaned from examination of thousands of documents in the Archivo General de Indias (Sevilla, Spain), particularly the section known as Papeles de Cuba. Service records and payroll accounts exist for many of the medical personnel, but individual correspondence and official reports supplement this information. In addition, there are records of the New Orleans Cabildo during the Spanish period (1769-1803) extant in the original and in transcript at the New Orleans Public Library. These were particularly useful for the period 1769-1795 for licensing of physicians, apothecaries and surgeons. The following printed materials supplement these basic documents.

OTHER PIONEER PHYSICIANS OF NEW ORLEANS

New Orleans today is one of the most celebrated medical centers of the world. Her fame in this regard can be attributed not only to the fine medical schools of the city but also in great measure to those dedicated physicians of pioneer days who worked so gallantly to stamp out pestilences, and to maintain the health of the inhabitants. The following partial listing of some of these men, who should be remembered, is taken mainly from a chapter written by Dr. Gayle Aiken in Henry Rightor's *Standard History of New Orleans*.

Forsyth, Dr. Gideon Comstock. Born in New London, Conn., May 4, 1780. Studied medicine at Columbia University; and practiced in Manhattan. In 1808 he married Mary Sally Ranson. At the insistence of his brother, Captain James Forsyth, he gave up practice in New York to settle in New Orleans and pursue his profession, where, with a few other doctors, he tried to organize a "Medico-Physico" Society, which gained him some favorable publicity; and due to his propagandizing for a "Quarantine Station" to prevent the spread of yellow fever, he was soon appointed the first Quarantine Doctor on the Mississippi River. The station was located below Braithwaite, La., and near what is called English Turn. He held this post for several years. But being eminently true to his profession and his responsibilities, he would not give "practique" to any vessel which had any type of fever or sickness aboard, with the result that many vessels were held at anchor. He ignored political pressure, and the merchants of New Orleans were out to scalp him. Finally the Governor of the State was compelled to abolish the station to please the merchants of New Orleans. Dr. Forsythe then purchased a plantation and manufactured rum from sugar cane, which added considerably to his income. His first wife died on his plantation, Scarsdale, in Plaquemines Parish, and he later married Elizabeth Procter Brooks. He died February 14, 1851. His son Lucius had several children, and among them was Hugh Laurel Forsyth, the father of Hewitt Laurie Forsyth of New Orleans.

Barton, Dr. Edward. Born in Virginia. He settled in New Orleans in the first or second decade of the 19th century. He made a careful study of yellow fever and wrote on that subject advocating the theory that under favorable meteorological and terrene (terrain) conditions (e.g. the digging and upturning of soil in the summer) the disease might originate in New Orleans. This theory was violently opposed by those believers in the invariable importation of yellow fever and the perfect efficiency of quarantine as a preventative. Dr. Barton filled the chair of Materia Medica and therapeutics in the University of Louisiana from 1835 to 1840. He died in 1867.

Bemiss, Dr. Samuel M. Was of Revolutionary stock. His father, thrown early upon his own resources, acquired a medical education in the face of countless difficulties. He settled in Kentucky where Samuel Bemiss was born. Samuel enjoyed the distinction of being the first matriculate of the University of New York where he graduated in 1845. He served as a surgeon in the Confederate army from 1861-1865. At the termination of the war, he returned to Louisville, but shortly afterward in 1866, he accepted the chair of Theory and Practice of Medicine in the University of Louisiana which he filled up to the day of his death, November 17, 1884. Dr. Bemiss was noted for conservative opinion and careful painstaking practice. In 1878 he was chairman of a commission appointed to investigate the origin and spread of yellow fever in the interior of Louisiana. He visited a number of infected towns and made a detailed report of his investigations. Dr. Bemiss was for some years the senior editor of the New Orleans Medical and Surgical Journal and his facile pen contributed to numerous scientific journals. He was a member of the American Medical Association, the College of Physicians and Surgeons of Louisville, of the Kentucky State Medical Society, the Boston Gynecological Society and of the State Medical Association of Louisiana.

Bickham, Dr. Charles Jasper. Born in Covington, Louisiana. M.A. from Southwestern University of Texas. Studied medicine in New Orleans where he graduated in 1856. He was a resident of New Orleans for 38 years. He assisted Dr. Stone in surgery, both in the doctor's own hospital and in the Charity Hospital. Dr. Bickham practiced medicine in Shreveport for a time, served as surgeon in the Confederate army during the war and afterwards settled permanently in New Orleans where he was noted for his urbanity to the younger members of the profession which led to an extensive consulting practice. He held the position of demonstrator of Anatomy at the University from 1867-1872; he was also an administrator of the Charity Hospital, a member of the Louisiana State Board of Health and a member of the Orleans Parish Medical Society.

Bruns, Dr. John Dickson. Born in Charleston, South Carolina, February 24, 1836. Graduated from the Medical College of South Carolina 1857 on which occasion his thesis entitled "Life, its Relations, Animal and Mental" won a prize of one hundred dollars. After traveling in the North and attending lectures there, Dr. Bruns returned to Charleston and edited the Charleston Medical Journal in 1858. He was a friend of Sims the novelist and also of the gentle poet Timrod, delighting both with his youthful enthusiasm and eloquence. He married in 1858. After the fall of the Confederacy, object of his allegiance, Dr. Bruns spent several months in Europe and in the autumn of 1866, accepted the chair of Physiology and Pathology at the Medical School of New Orleans. He was later elected professor of Practice of Medicine at the Charity Hospital Medical School. He was associated for several years with Drs. Choppin, Beard and Brickell in practice. His pen was ever active and his poems are full of chaste and delicate fancy. His most brilliant scientific papers appeared in the Southern Journal of Medical Science (1867) and in the New Orleans Medical and Surgical Journal (1880). His poetry was praised: " 'Morturi Salutamus' " is a poem, said the *Times-Democrat*, "which we fully believe deserves a permanent place in the gallery of English chef d'oeuvres".

Choppin, Dr. Samuel. Born in Baton Rouge in 1828. Graduated from the University of Louisiana in 1849. He spent two years in Paris to complete his medical education and while there witnessed the coup d'etat of Louis Napoleon in 1851, and narrowly escaped with his life upon one occasion, being but one of a defenseless crowd which was suddenly and unexpectedly fired upon by French soldiers. On his return to New Orleans he was appointed demonstrator of Anatomy in the Medical College, a position which he held for five years. During the same period he was house surgeon of the Charity Hospital. He devoted much time to the literature of medicine and was associate editor of the New Orleans Medical and Hospital Gazette which printed his "Notes on Syphilis". In conjunction with Drs. E. D. Fenner, D. W. Brickell and C. Beard, Dr. Choppin took an active part in organizing the New Orleans School of Medicine in 1856. He served as medical inspector, and surgeon-in-chief to General Beauregard and was present at the siege of Charleston and of Petersburg. Upon his return to New Orleans after the war, he formed a partnership with Dr. C. Beard. His sympathies were enlisted in the struggle of his native state with the radical despotism and he was one of the leaders and organizers of the revolution of September 14, 1874.

Dr. Choppin was president of the Board of Health in 1875. He made a gallant struggle to protect the community from the invasion of yellow fever but failed in 1878. The treachery of seeming friends and the misrepresentations of the press, embittered his last years. He died of pneumonia on May 2, 1880.

Fenner, Dr. Erasmus Darwin. Inherited his love of medicine from his father, a distinguished physician from a fine North Carolina family. He graduated from the University of Transylvania, Kentucky and began his practice in Jackson, Tennessee. He married in 1832 but lost his young wife in 1837 and cherished her memory with unswerving fidelity throughout his long and useful life. In 1840 he moved to New Orleans with his little son to whose education he devoted all of his leisure hours. Then ensued some years of poverty and obscurity through which the doctor struggled toward the prominence and success which he finally achieved. In 1844 he published, in collaboration with Dr. A. Hester, The New Orleans Medical Journal. So low were the funds of these two editors that the Journal was published on credit but each number somehow managed to pay its own way until the Journal was absorbed into the New Orleans Medical and Surgical Journal in 1848, this being a publication to which Dr. Fenner contributed largely and brilliantly. His most valued articles were two accounts of the yellow fever prevailing in 1846 and 1848 and a pamphlet entitled "History of the Epidemic of Yellow Fever in New Orleans in 1853". Dr. Fenner was an ardent advocate of sanitary measures whose advice was indifferently received. The earnest object of his life was achieved when he established with the aid of kindred spirits, the New Orleans School of Medicine in 1856.

Dr. Fenner's eloquence and energy secured for the students and faculty of the school all the privileges of the Charity Hospital. He also procured from the Legislature an appropriation of $20,000 for enlarging the buildings and increasing the museum. The school opened in 1856 with a class of seventy-six students. It closed its doors at the beginning of the civil war with two hundred and forty-seven students, many of whom shouldered their muskets until the close of the struggle permitted the survivors to resume their interrupted studies. The school was utilized as a Negro school during the Federal domination but was later reorganized and reopened in 1865. After a few sessions and the death of Dr. Fenner, the New Orleans School of Medicine ceased to exist.

Dr. Fenner originated the Louisiana Hospital in Richmond during the war and refused to take the oath of allegiance for which he was punished by General Butler by being banished. He then went to Mobile where he remained until the end of the war.

He returned to New Orleans when peace was established, resumed his extensive practice and was pursuing his career with unabated energy when he suddenly succumbed to fever on May 4, 1866. Dr. Fenner was known as a man of sociable and lovable character and was remarkably devoted to his children. He left an honored name worthily borne by his son Judge Charles E. Fenner.

Holcombe, Dr. William H. Well known for his services toward the cause of homeopathy (treating a disease by administration of minute doses of a remedy that would in healthy persons produce symptoms of the disease treated), Dr. Holcombe was born in Lynchburg, Virginia, May 29, 1825. He was of an old Virginia family, his grandfather having served in the Continental Army. His father was a distinguished physician of the old school and young Holcombe was sent to the University of Pennsylvania where he graduated in 1847. He moved to Cincinnati and it was there, during an epidemic of Asiatic cholera that he became interested in the study of homeopathy. The marked success he met with in the experimental use of this field induced him to devote himself to this new school of medicine and he soon became one of its most talented disciples. Dr. Holcombe moved to Natchez, Mississippi in 1852 where he and Dr. Davis, his partner, were both appointed surgeons and physicians to the Mississippi State Hospital. In 1864 he relocated in New Orleans where he made his home until his death on November 28, 1893. He was chairman of a yellow fever commission in 1878 and published an excellent report of the work done during the epidemic of that year. Dr. Holcombe was for many years co-editor of the North American Journal of Homeopathy and was president of the American Institute of Homeopathy in 1876. In 1852 he published "The Scientific Basis of Homeopathy" and in 1856 "Yellow Fever and the Homeopathic Treatment". He was the author of a number of medical treatises, of two volumes of poetry and of eight religious works embodying the doctrines of Swedenborg. His last literary composition, "The Truth About Homeopathy", was completed only a few days before his death when he succumbed quite suddenly to heart disease.

Holt, Dr. Joseph. Was the real inventor of the present system of quarantine for yellow fever. In 1884 Dr. Holt substituted a solution of bichloride of mercury for carbolic acid and obtained from the Legislature an appropriation of $30,000 to put into operation his plan of maritime sanitation. In 1885 an apparatus was erected, consisting of a sulphur furnace with a steam propelled fan attached, connected with a 12" galvanized conductor leading to the hold of the vessel. Dr. Holt also built a heating chamber for the disinfection of clothing, bedding, etc.

Jones, Dr. Joseph. Occupies a notable position as an authority on yellow fever. Dr. Jones devoted years to the most careful and minute researches and his work entitled "Medical and Surgical Memoirs" contains a wealth of information, statistics and scientific data. Dr. Jones was president of the State Board of Health assuming office in April 1880. He was also connected with the University for many years as a professor of Chemistry. His range was very wide — he was a leading archaeologist of the South and had a collection of rare and antique arms, pottery, etc. which is justly an object of pride to the whole city.

Luzenburg, Dr. C. A. Born of Austrian parents in Verona, Italy, 1805. His father moved to Germany where this talented youth received his education and learned so well that the mayor of Wissenburg is said to have removed his hat in the presence of the elder Luzenburg saying "Sir, I must uncover my head before the man who owns such a son." Dr. Luzenburg emigrated to Philadelphia in 1819. Becoming deeply interested in tropical fevers, he decided to settle in New Orleans where the field for study would be varied and extensive. He settled in the southern metropolis in 1829 and was shortly thereafter elected house surgeon of the Charity Hospital.

Dr. Luzenburg devoted his talents and energy to combating yellow fever, the scourge which then visited the city almost every year. He revolutionized the medical practice of the day. Instead of using calomel and purgatives, he treated the disease by general and localized bleeding. This method was met by violent opposition, and fierce invective was resorted to in the medical journals of the day to combat this heresy. Dr. Luzenburg was the first practitioner in New Orleans who excluded light from the apartments of small-pox patients, having noticed its baleful influence in the disfiguring effect of the malady.

In 1832 the Doctor contracted a wealthy marriage with Mrs. Mary Ford and enjoyed an extensive European tour, visiting all of the better hospitals studying, comparing, and analyzing with inexhaustible energy. His return to New Orleans was greeted with enthusiasm. The charitable impulses of his nature led him to devote two hours daily to the service of the poor and to offer, during an epidemic, to treat all indigent Germans gratis.

With the wealth now at his disposal he built a hospital on Elysian Fields called the Franklin Infirmary. The operations performed by Dr. Luzenburg entitled him to rank among the foremost surgeons of the century. In removing a cancer he made a complete extirpation of the parotid gland; the patient, a man of 62, survived and lived in good health for several years. He also made an excision of six inches of the ileum and distinguished himself by tying the primitive iliac artery for the cure of an aneurism of the external iliac. Dr. Luzenburg's specialty was the removal of cataracts and many grateful eyes owed their sight to his skill.

Dr. Luzenburg was Dean of the Medical College of Louisiana which he originated, delivering lectures in the old State House on Canal Street and giving demonstrations in Charity Hospital. Dr. Luzenburg also filled the chairs of Anatomy and Surgery in 1835. This outspoken man of strong character, was persecuted and maligned by many enemies, and his life was saddened by their machinations. He withdrew voluntarily from the College but was expelled from the Physic-Medical Society and sued for *mal praxis* in the Criminal Court. The suit was carried to the Supreme Court of Louisiana where Dr. Luzenburg was acquitted. He endured these trials with dignity and courage, turning a deaf ear to those who counselled flight or withdrawal from the scene of so many labors. He remained and now devoted himself entirely to the Charity Hospital. In spite of opposition he was elected an administrator and afterwards vice-president, a position he held for the rest of his life.

In 1839 Dr. Luzenburg founded the Society of Natural History and Sciences and, in 1843, he formed and incorporated the Louisiana Medico-Chirurgical Society. In 1843 he was also physician to the Marine Hospital. Dr. Luzenburg's health failed in 1848 and he left the city to find strength at a Virginia spring but died enroute in Cincinnati on July 15, 1848.

Mercer, Dr. William Newton. Born in 1792 in Cecil County, Maryland. He had every educational advantage during his youth and was for several years a pupil of Dr. Benjamin Rush at the University of Pennsylvania. After graduating with honors, Dr. Mercer was appointed assistant surgeon in the army at about the beginning of the War of 1812. He came to New Orleans with the army in 1816 but was soon ordered to Natchez, where he resided for some years, winning a high position through his sterling character and lofty integrity. Dr. Mercer returned to New Orleans in 1843 and soon became one of its most honored citizens. St. Anna's Asylum, one of our most worthy charities, was liberally endowed by him in memory of his lovely daughter who died in her twentieth year. In conjunction with Dr. Duncan of Natchez, Mr. Mercer paid an installment due on the home of Henry Clay, who would have been involved in bankruptcy but for the timely aid so generously tendered to him. Dr. Mercer was loyal to the Union but he shared all of the hardships of his fellow citizens during the war and was able to assist and protect many unfortunate families. Dr. Mercer lived in New Orleans for some years after the war, the type of a generation of courteous and noble gentlemen.

Mercier, Dr. Alfred. Born 1816, died 1894. A graduate of the College of Louis Le Grand, having received his medical education in France. He was the secretary of the Athenée Louisianaise and a leading spirit in literary circles, being a distinguished Latin, Greek and Italian scholar. "The Rose of Smyrna", "The Hermit of Niagra", "St. Ybars Plantation" and "Lydia" are among the most charming productions of his pen.

Miles, Dr. Albert B. One of the most esteemed physicians of late years. A native of Alabama, born in 1852. An education begun in the Gordon Institute of Arkansas was completed at the University of Virginia in 1870 when he graduated at the age of 18. Coming to New Orleans in 1872, he began the study of medicine and became a resident student at Charity Hospital in 1873. He graduated in 1875 and was at once elected demonstrator of Anatomy in the medical department of the University. After filling the position of visiting physician in the hospital and of assistant house surgeon, he was appointed physician in charge of the Hotel Dieu, and in 1882, house surgeon of Charity Hospital which position he held until his death of typhoid fever August 5, 1894. He made a gallant struggle for life and when informed that the end was near, exclaimed "So soon" — a sentiment soon echoed by the whole community. Dr. Miles was a member of the New Orleans Medical and Surgical Association of the Orleans Parish Medical Association and of the Louisiana State Medical Society.

Perry, Dr. Alfred W. In 1874 designed and constructed a machine for pumping sulphuric acid gas into the holds of ships. The yellow fever quarantine detention was relaxed by an act of the Legislature in 1876 and vessels allowed to come to the city after a brief stay of a few hours at the station.

Richardson, Dr. T. G. Born in Lexington, Kentucky, 1827. Received a complete medical education at the University of Louisville and afterwards enjoyed years of profitable intercourse with the celebrated Dr. Gross whose private pupil he was. He was appointed demonstrator of Anatomy in the medical department of the University of Louisville immediately after his graduation in 1848. He accepted in 1856 the chair of Anatomy in the Pennsylvania Medical College. He acquired a professional reputation at the age of 29 with the publication of a text book entitled "Richardson's Elements of Human Anatomy." While in Philadelphia Dr. Richardson edited with Dr. Gross, the "North American Medico-Chirurgical Review." He moved to New Orleans in 1858 to occupy the chair of Anatomy at Tulane University which he occupied until 1872. Dr. Richardson then accepted the chair of Surgery, which he occupied for 17 years. He was dean of the medical department of Tulane from 1865-1885, and was professor emeritus of Surgery until his death. Dr. Richardson was president of the American Medical Association during the year 1877-78 and presided at the session held in Buffalo. As a surgeon of General Bragg's staff, Dr. Richardson followed the fortunes of war from 1862 to 1865, then returning to his home. A terrible domestic bereavement was added to the sorrows of the patriot; he lost his wife and three children in the explosion and wreck of a Mississippi steamboat. These sorrows, endured with courage and submission, probably emphasized the cold reserve and dignity of his manner. His friend Dr. Edmond Souchon tells a story which illustrates his courage and devotion to duty. Being called to a patient who was bleeding profusely, he introduced the tiny silver canula into the vein at the elbow and in the simplest way told Dr. Souchon, his assistant, to introduce the other end into his (Dr. Richardson's) vein, thus giving his own blood to restore the patient, but in vain. Dr. Richardson died on May 26, 1892, but a notable memorial was erected to him by his second wife, Mrs. Ida A. Richardson, in the superbly fitted medical college, for the building of which she donated one hundred thousand dollars.

Smyth, Dr. A. W. Held for many years the position of

house surgeon in the Charity Hospital to which he was elected in 1862. Dr. Smyth's unusual mechanical gifts led to the introduction of many improvements in the domestic arrangements of the hospital. But his fame rests securely upon the fact that he was the first surgeon who successfully performed the operation of tying the innominata, the vertebral, and other arteries for the cure of subclavian aneurism. Dr. Smyth was a graduate of the Medical College of Louisiana. An Irishman by birth, he returned to his native land to spend his declining years.

Stone, Dr. Warren. Professor of Surgery at the University of Louisiana for 35 years and surgeon of the Charity Hospital for 39 years. He was born in St. Albans, Vermont in 1808. Dr. Stone's education was conducted by private tutors and he became a pupil of Dr. Twitchell, an eminent surgeon and physician of Keene, New Hampshire. He frequently declared that he was indebted to Dr. Twitchell for the most valuable portion of his extensive professional knowledge. He was an ardent student and when he graduated from the medical school in Pittsfield, Mass., in 1831, he was thoroughly equipped in all the various branches of medicine. In 1832 he started from Boston by sea for New Orleans but the brig *Amelia* met with violent storms, cholera appeared among the passengers and crew and the vessel finally ran aground on Folly Island, at the entrance to Charleston harbor. The passengers were supplied with all needful and medicines by the generous people of Charleston and Dr. Thomas Hunt, a distinguished physician, rendered devoted attention to the sick. The *Amelia* was burned as a necessary sanitary measure but another vessel was soon chartered to convey passengers and crew to their destination. Dr. Stone at last landed in New Orleans, friendless and poor, at a time when yellow fever and cholera were both raging in the city. Through the kindness of Dr. Cenas, young Stone received some employment in connection with the Charity Hospital. His unusual ability and industry soon made a favorable impression upon all around him.

When Dr. Hunt, with whom he had formed a warm friendship during the days on Folly Island, moved to New Orleans from Charleston and was appointed resident surgeon at the hospital, he secured for Dr. Stone the position of assistant to Dr. Picton. So clearly were his abilities demonstrated in this post that he was appointed resident surgeon of the hospital in 1836. He was elected lecturer on Anatomy in 1836 and in January 1837, professor of Anatomy. Upon the resignation of Professor Luzenburg he became professor of Surgery. In November of 1849, Dr. Stone operated successfully in a case of traumatic aneurism of the vertebral artery, by incising the sac, turning out the coagulum and controlling the artery by a graduated compress. He also enjoyed the humane distinction of being the first in New Orleans to use chloroform for the alleviation of suffering on February 25, 1847.

Dr. Stone built and conducted a private infirmary at the corner of Canal and Claiborne Streets from 1859 to 1867. Dr. William Kennedy, a prominent physician of the day, was associted with Dr. Stone in this and although much good was achieved, the enterprise was financially unsuccessful and was finally abandoned. At the outbreak of the Civil War, Dr. Stone was appointed Confederate surgeon-general of the State of Louisiana. He was present at the battles of Bull Run and Shiloh and devoted his fine surgical skill to the alleviation of the pain suffered by the wounded soldiers. When New Orleans was in the hands of the Federals, he was sent to Fort Jackson where he treated Union soldiers. But gladly as he rendered aid to the suffering, regardless of sectional or political feeling, he was never "reconstructed" but remained to the end an euthusiastic Democrat, the devoted friend of Jefferson Davis. Dr. Stone lost the sight in one eye in 1841 from an inflammation contracted from a patient. Dr. Stone was a frequent contributor to the Medical Journal. Among his important articles, were, "The Treatment of Wounded Arteries", "Ligation of the Common Iliac Artery" and "Inflammation". The physician died December 6, 1872.

Taxile, Dr. Settled in New Orleans in 1841. Practiced until his death in 1857. He was a pioneer of homeopathy (i.e., the treating of a disease by administration of minute doses of a remedy that would in healthy persons produce symptoms of the disease being treated).

THE YELLOW FEVER PERIOD

Any schoolboy knows the names of the great generals of history, and likewise of the famous pirates and criminals who became so notorious as to have their infamy dramatized. But it is doubtful that more than a small number of educated adults can remember that it was around the middle of the nineteenth century that anesthesia, one of humanity's greatest blessings, was discovered by Drs. Horace Wells, Crawford W. Long, W. T. G. Morton, and Sir J. Y. Simpson. Other physicians and scientists contributed greatly toward perfecting the substance and applying it but these men were the pioneers in the field. Similarly, it is doubtful that many people know anything of the men who were responsible for eradicating yellow fever, which plagued New Orleans and other areas of the nation for nearly one hundred years. New Orleans has a semi-tropical climate, and here the early settlers found that the maintenance of health was a baffling problem.

The first appearance of yellow fever is still controversial. The disease was not recognized as such by the early inhabitants. In his book on "Pestilence" Noah Webster said that when the white man arrived in New England in 1620 some of the Indian tribes had been reduced from thirty or forty thousand to a few hundred "as the result of a terrible fever." Those affected "bled by the nose and turned yellow, like a garment of that color, which they pointed out as an illustration." The disease was not, therefore, confined to Louisiana and the Gulf Coast. Margaret Haughery reported that it struck Baltimore in 1822, and both of her parents and thousands of other people died of it. It is very probable that yellow fever was prevalent on the shores of the Gulf of Mexico when European settlers arrived, for the sailors of Columbus and those bound for South American countries reported that they were attacked by a violent fever in the West Indies. Cortez found (in 1519) that the Aztecs suffered from a similar disease, which sometimes depopulated half of their cities. LaSalle said there was a deadly fever lurking on the shores of the Mississippi, which caused the death of many of his soldiers. As early as 1647, Dr. Richard Vines, a planter in the Barbados, recorded "an absolute plague of fever." And Mr. Hughes said, in his "Natural History of Barbados," that Dr. Gamble found "pestilential fever or Kenfal fever in the Barbados (in 1691) to be 'most fatal.' " There can be little doubt that the disease described by these authorities was in fact yellow fever, which had visited this part of the world centuries before European settlers arrived. This fever did not appear in Brazil until 1849 (so far as known), and it struck Peru in 1855. In 1820 it appeared on the west coast of Africa. In Georgetown (British Guiana) 69 percent of the garrison died of the disease in 1840. The disease found its way to various ports of Spain, and Cadiz suffered five epidemics in the 18th century.

This fever was known in some parts of the world as "fievre de Siam" and was believed to have spread from the Far East to the Western World but Dr. Joseph Jones, an eminent authority, declared that yellow fever had been "sporadical in two continents since men born under a cold zone were exposed, in low torrid regions, to miasmatic atmosphere." There was apparently more than one type of fever known as "yellow," and the familiar type generally known as "yellow fever," which was believed to have been brought to Louisiana and the whole Gulf Coast by French settlers from the West Indies, was here long before the French arrived. The disease was here when LaSalle came, and was especially prevalent in Louisiana during the summer of 1701 and also the summer of 1704. The Chevalier Tonti, Le Vasseur, the Jesuit Donge, and thirty soldiers died of it in 1704. The Sieur de Sauvole contracted this disease while in Biloxi in 1702, and recovered but was compelled to return to France to restore his health. He died in Havana in 1706. In 1729 the scourge invaded Mobile, and Bienville lost many soldiers.

THE PLAGUE IN NEW ORLEANS

Yellow fever continued to plague New Orleans for many years. Its virulence varied, and the number of cases from year to year also varied. For instance, there were no cases reported in 1787 and 1788 but an epidemic occurred in 1796, when the population of New Orleans was 8,756. Some historians say there were epidemics before that time. Dr. Albert E. Fossier says, however, in his book, "New Orleans — the Glamour Period, 1800-1840," "careful research proves that such opinions are not based on facts." It is most difficult to determine the exact or nearly the exact number of cases, for the writers on the subject do not agree. The New Orleans City Guide states that from June to October in 1853 there were 7,189 deaths from yellow fever. In one day, August 31 of the same year, there were 230 deaths reported. There were some cases every year following the terrible epidemic of 1853 but an epidemic occurred again in 1878, and, according to the New Orleans City Guide, there were 3,800 cases. Dr. Fossier says that he found from statistical records that in the period of 1822 to 1844 there were 9,637 cases and 3,787 deaths. But he explains that these figures are only approximate, yet accurate enough for comparison. He says that the epidemics of yellow fever were not of equal virulence, and in some years it was fatal in nearly every case, whereas in other years the disease was of medium intensity, with a low death rate. Frequently the epidemics were so mild that nearly every patient recovered.

DISCOVERY OF CAUSE, TREATMENT, AND ELIMINATING THE DISEASE

In 1881, after many papers had been written by eminent physicians of New Orleans concerning the cause and treatment of yellow fever, Dr. Charles Finlay of Havana advanced the theory that mosquitoes were the carriers of the infection. The particular mosquito selected as guilty by Dr. Finlay was the stegomyia fasciata, a black one, with silver markings on the thorax. Physicians in New Orleans and Cuba became greatly interested in this theory, and began a serious investigation. They caught specimens of this insect and allowed them to feed on persons established in a special camp with other susceptible persons as a control. Those bitten developed the fever, the others (protected from them) did not.

The people of Louisiana were jubilant over this discovery, and those who didn't have wire screened doors (few had) put up mosquito bars around their beds, i.e., a mosquito netting. Although they didn't know it at the time, this was the best possible protection, for the Stegomyia must have a feed of blood in order to lay her eggs, and she lays them three days after. Before she lays her eggs (when she has not sucked yellow fever blood or any blood, for that matter), she strikes both night and day but after that period she strikes only at night. Persons bitten in the day-time did not develop yellow fever, while those bitten at night did. It was noticed that Europeans visited infected areas with impunity if they did not spend the night there. It was stated by Drs. Marchoux and Simond that an infected mosquito "transmits the parasite to her eggs, the progeny proving infective."

An American commission was appointed in 1901, which consisted of Drs. Walter Reed, James Carroll, A. Agramonte, and Jesse Lazear, to study the disease further, and devise means of stamping it out. They were eminently successful. A vigorous campaign was instituted in the United States and Havana to eliminate mosquitoes. In Cuba this campaign was under the direction of Major W. C. Gorgas of the United States army, who was chief sanitary officer of Havana (the U. S. had treaty rights in Cuba from 1899 to 1934).

It was John R. Kissinger, a private in the U. S. Army, who offered himself as a "guinea pig" in the experiment to prove that the mosquito, Stegomyia fasciata, carried the deadly yellow fever germ. He allowed mosquitoes to bite him until he contracted the disease, and although he recovered the fever impaired his health, and he was confined to a wheelchair for twelve years. Finally (in 1911) Congress voted him a grant of $100.00 a month. Major Walter Reed said: "In my opinion this exhibition of moral courage has never been surpassed in the annals of the Army of the United States.

(From an article in the Times-Picayune's DIXIE by Paul V. D. Hoysradt.)

TREATMENT

Dr. Fossier says that "as there was no specific treatment, the physicians had to resort to empiric methods." Physicians were baffled in their efforts to find a cure for a disease having so high a death rate. Dr. Musdovoi devised a medicine containing cinchona, tartar emetic, cream of tartar, and an ammonia salt. Drs. Gros and Geradin treated the disease by bleeding, and administering mild evacuants, drinks with cream of tartar, citrus fruit, and buttermilk. They recommended luke warm baths, and rubbing the body with lemons and vinegar. Dr. Sternberg introduced a system of treatment by alkalis to counteract the hyperacidity of the intestinal contents and increase the flow of urine. Of 301 whites treated by this method only 7.3% died, and of 72 blacks all recovered. Mercurial treatment was controversial among doctors. It is said that some patients died of the treatment rather than of the disease. Dr. Edward Barton wrote a paper in 1832 opposing this method of treatment. Negroes, for an unknown reason, did not contract the disease as readily as whites, and nearly all recovered.

Asiatic cholera has also played a very important part in the history of New Orleans. The first authentic record we have of its appearance in this city was in 1832. An epidemic of yellow fever already prevailed, when the horror of the situation was deepened by the announcement that cholera had been reported, a case having been discovered on October 25. It spread with alarming rapidity, and out of a total of 8,090 deaths that year from all causes, 4,340 were ascribed to cholera. This was the darkest year in the history of New Orleans, the death rate reaching the enormous proportion of 147.10 per 1,000. The population at this time was 55,084, and more than one-seventh succumbed to disease. The following year, '33, was also marked by a cholera visitation; this disease claimed 1,000 victims out of a total of 4,976 deaths. It reappeared in 1848, destroying 1,646 inhabitants. The city was infested with this malady for seven years; in 1849 it raged in an alarming manner, carrying off 3,176 victims. This was its last virulent visitation. In 1850, '51, '52, '53 and '55 it was heroically combatted by the medical profession, and many able treatises were written on the subject. The gradual disappearance of cholera has been, at least, one hopeful feature of the pathological history of the city.

Small-pox, also, committed great ravages among the early settlers of Louisiana and before the introduction of vaccination. Thirty-five years after the foundation of the colony, historians notice the prevalence and fatality of this disease. Vaccination was introduced a little later than 1802, over objections of the Catholic priests, and since that time, up to 1861-1865, New Orleans was almost exempt from destructive epidemics of small-pox. In 1849 the deaths from small-pox were 133; in 1857, 103; in 1858, 108. During the civil war the disease committed greater ravages, the deaths in 1864 being 605; in 1866, 613; and in 1870, 528. 1877 was the year in which small-pox reached its height, 1,099 deaths from it being reported. During the forty years extending from 1844 to 1883, there was a total of 7,070 deaths from this cause.

What Is a Creole?

CREOLE is probably the most controversial word in the English language. Webster's Dictionary gives the definition as (1) A person of French or Spanish descent born and reared in a colonial or remote region, especially a tropical region. (2) A white person descended from the French or Spanish settlers of Louisiana and the Gulf States, who preserve their characteristic speech and culture. A Negro born in America—more properly a Creole Negro. (3) A person of mixed Creole and Negro blood speaking a dialect of French and Spanish; a half-breed . . . Adj. Designating or relating to a Creole; of Creole blood and culture. (2) Designating or relating to a Creole or Creoles; as, a Negro dialect.

This definition, if it is a definition at all, is most confusing. For instance, a simple definition of the word "Knickerbocher" is: **A name which came to be used as a term for all early Dutch settlers.** It does not mean to indicate classic distinction or any degree of culture. A Knickerbocher could be of a high or low station, as long as he was of the early Dutch settlers of New York. The word Creole, in fact, means nothing, for it can be used in a laudatory sense or in a derogatory sense.

The Creoles of the prosperous days before the Civil War, says Henry Rightor, "at once kept an eye to material wants of life, and cultivated the most princely and refined society of the day, educating their sons in Paris, their daughters in the refining and spiritualizing atmosphere of Catholic convents, and so producing a race of fiery, spirited, chivalrous, cultured men and delicately beautiful, modest and charmingly feminine women."

The Encyclopedia Americana, published in 1835, edited by Francis Lieber, says: CREOLE (from the Spanish **Criollo)** is the name which was originally given to all descendants of Spaniards born in America and the West Indies. It is also used for the descendants of other Europeans, as French, Danes, in which we say FrenchCreole, Danish Creole . . . In the West Indies the Creoles have always enjoyed equal rights with native Europeans. Before the declaration of independence by the colonies of Spanish America there existed marked lines of distinction between the different classes, founded on difference of birth. The CHAPETONES were Europeans by birth and first in rank and power; the Creoles were second; the Mulattoes and mestizos (descendants of white and black or white and Indian parents) formed a third class; Negroes and Indians the fourth.

If, as stated in the foregoing (definition) "founded on difference of birth, the Creoles were second in rank and power" in the West Indies, they were (and are today) rated as first in Louisiana. It is inconceivable that there were ever any such classifications anywhere. What would make an individual born in Europe superior to one born in the West Indies! It would be as well to say that a man born of Latin European parents in the hilly sections of Mississippi or Louisiana is a hillbilly but if he migrated to the West Indies (or to South Louisiana) he would become a Creole, and (if in the West Indies) would be of second rank, irrespective of his acquirements in education. Alexander Hamilton was born in the West Indies of European parents, and would, therefore, be classed as a Creole but obviously he did not fall into the second class rank. His father was a prominent merchant, and his mother was a French Huguenot. Empress Josephine was a Creole of Martinique.

Henry Rightor, in his Standard History of New Orleans, offers the most sensible definition of the Creole. He says: "The term Creole in its Louisiana sense has been accepted throughout the civilized world as among the proudest warranties of a gentle, cultured, patrician people to be found on the Western Hemisphere."

The term in Louisiana has a wide meaning and a varied use. There are Creole eggs, Creole tomatoes, Creole cattle, Creole corn, Creole ponies, Creole peppers, and Creole cottonade. This term came to be applied to animals and vegetables. When a Negro or any servant either sold or delivered them, he felt it necessary to explain that they came from his Creole master, and were therefore Creole-produced; that is, they were not imported but were a home product. Thus they were fresh and superior to anything shipped in, which had probably suffered in transit.

In 1886 a CREOLE ASSOCIATION was formed in New Orleans, the purpose of which was to identify the Creoles of Louisiana, and to show that, like the Knickerbochers of New York and the French Protestants (or Huguenots) of South Carolina, they were considered the "very best in the land." Colonel Charles Villeré, vice president of the Association, made a brilliant speech on the subject, and it was published in newspapers and magazines throughout the country. Apparently there was at that time a group or class of people (perhaps new settlers from the eastern states) who were prejudiced against the Creoles, for A. L. Roman, Recording Secretary of the Association wrote: "It is far from our purpose to deny that among the Creoles, as well as all other races, there are ignorant and slothful people. On the contrary, one of the objects embraced in this program is to awaken that very class of our people to the necessity of education and to the demands of progress. But at the same time we intend to demonstrate and protest against the injustice of selecting the weakest of a race, and to hold it up as a type of that race. Why should writers of romance and of contemporaneous history seek their models of Creoles from the wild and unimproved prairies of the Attakapas and the Opelousas, while they turn their faces from the many representative Creoles in this city and other portions of the State, who yield to none in intelligence, in patriotism and in refinement."

We shall never know exactly when or how the word, "Creole," originated. It once had a strict and definite meaning but became one of the most abused and misunderstood words in the English language. The educated Creole is proud of the name, for he knows that in its true sense it means the first settlers who came to Louisiana, blazed the trail and built the country. But a stranger coming to Louisiana feels that he should use the word with caution, for he has heard several interpretations of it, and cannot be sure which is correct.

A CREOLE FAMILY AT THE OPERA. From an article in "Every Saturday," the issue of July 15, 1871.

The German Coast

In 1717 the "Western Company," headed by John Law, received a trade monopoly in the colony of Louisiana for a period of twenty-five years. It was granted the right to issue for sale an unlimited number of shares of stock. And it was also authorized to give land to settlers on certain conditions, as it saw fit. But in consideration of these privileges it obligated itself to bring into the territory 6,000 white people and 3,000 Negroes during the life of the franchise. The shares of the company sold readily in France, for it was supposed (or John Law led the people to believe) that there was an inexhaustible supply of minerals throughout this land, and that the rich alluvial soil could produce crops to bring immediate wealth to those occupied in farming or in backing the producers. This was in a sense true but the enormous wealth was not to be available for more than a hundred years. The wilderness had to be cleared, the sulphur and salt mines had to be located, and methods of refining their products found; the oil wells had to be discovered, and the uses of oil and its by-products had to be found.

John Law was not unaware of the travail the new settlers

would suffer, and he wisely decided to persuade a number of Germans (mainly from Alsace-Lorraine where there was much poverty) to settle in the territory, for he felt the Germans were hardier than the French. In a booklet printed in German, the following paragraph appeared:

> "The land is filled with gold, silver, copper, and lead mines. If one wishes to hunt for mines he need only to go into the country of the Natchitoches. There he will surely draw pieces of silver mines out of the earth. After these mines we will hunt for herbs and plants for the apothecaries. The savages will make them known to us. Soon we shall find healing remedies for the most dangerous wounds, yes, also, so they say, infallible ones for the fruits of love."

The enigmatic C. C. Robin, who wrote about his travels to Louisiana in 1803-1805, at the end of the colonial period and on the eve of American rule, described the Germans of early Louisiana as follows:

"These Germans living among the French have retained their aciturn character, their language and their manners. They do not have that open and affectionate countenance of the French. They are stingy but well behaved. They work their own farms, without Negroes, and although originally northern they have become well acclimated. Yellow fever never bothers them because they work. This malady strikes those who in New Orleans live in inactivity or in the too active state of passion and intemperance.

"These Germans, who are the food suppliers of the city, (as I have already observed) live well, without however having made any fortunes. This is hardly astonishing when we consider that the city market is not large, that the price of meat has always been low, and that the artificial restrictions of commerce have prevented the development of other outlets."

(Source: C. C. Robin, *Voyage to Louisiana*. Trans. by Stuart O. Landry, Jr. (New Orleans: Pelican Publishing Co., 1966, 114.)

J. Hanno Deiler in his book, *The Settlement of the German Coast of Louisiana and the Creoles of German Descent*, says he found this booklet in a little shop in Exchange Alley, New Orleans, and bought it for the Fisk Library. It was printed by J. Friedrich Gleditschen's seel, Sohn Leipsic, in 1720, and was widely distributed in Germany, Alsace and Lorraine, as well as in Holland, and in sections of Germany which had not recovered from the terrible Thirty Years' War (1618-1648) and later from the invasion of Louis XIV's troops in taking away portions of Alsace and Lorraine from the German Empire. Thousands of people, therefore, emigrated to Louisiana in the hope of getting rich, and living in great comfort, free from political tyranny, and free to worship in any religion. Such glowing prospects were hard to resist.

A letter published in this book, from a Louisiana settler to his wife, says: "I betook myself to where they are beginning to build the capitol, New Orleans. Its circumference will be one mile. The houses are poor and low, as at home with us in the country. They are covered with large pieces of bark and strong reeds. Everybody dresses as he pleases, but all very poorly. One's outfit consists of a suit of clothes, bed, tables, and trunks. Tapestry and fine beds are entirely unknown. The people sleep the whole night in open air. I am as safe in the most distant part of the town as in a citadel. Although I live among savages and Frenchmen, I am in no danger. People trust one another so much that they leave gates and doors open."

Historians (especially German historians) say that as a result of this promotion campaign, 10,000 Germans emigrated to Louisiana. And it is said (with little proof) there were also thousands of people from Switzerland and Holland who emigrated to Louisiana after hearing the fabulous tales of wealth, easy living, and religious freedom. It is probably doubtful that as many as 10,000 left Germany during so short a period as stated by most historians but it is certain that a much smaller number arrived. Chevalier Guy Soniat in his *Synopsis of the History of Louisiana* says that 6,000 Germans left Europe for Louisiana. But only about 2,000 reached the colony, and they did not all settle there; some moved on to Alabama and Florida. We are bound to suppose, therefore, that 4,000 persons died on the ships and were buried at sea, all within a short period of time; and still they came, knowing of the hazards of the trip. The first German emigrants landed at Biloxi, and it is said that more than a thousand died of starvation and disease before they could establish a home and produce crops. Many wished to return to their homes in Europe but were unable to do so. The return trip would have been slightly safer, for buccaneers who invaded the seas, mainly attacked vessels enroute from Europe to America, for these ships were always loaded with provisions, arms, ammunition, and money for the colonists. Deiler says that in 1721 a French ship with 300 very sick Germans "on board was captured by buccaneers near the Bay of Samana in San Domingo." What happened to them is unknown.

John Law did not, however, depend entirely upon the Germans and Hollanders to populate Louisiana. He succeeded in persuading many respectable French families to emigrate. Some of them were aristocrats or even of the nobility. But no historian has failed to mention that he also gathered up in Paris shiploads of mendicants, prostitutes, people imprisoned for real or supposed crimes, and people who wished to escape from their creditors. It is difficult to determine how many such individuals arrived in Louisiana. It is certain, however, that only a small number remained in the colony, for being naturally weak in character, and improvident, they could not stand the travail of the pioneer. Many died of starvation or disease, and a good number of them either returned to Europe or moved on to larger cities of the Atlantic coast. The Chevalier Champigny in his *Memoire La. Haye* (in 1776) said, "You cannot find twenty of these vagabond families in Louisiana now." He regarded the Germans and the Canadians as the founders of all our establishments in Louisiana.

It cannot be said that the German emigrants settled only in Louisiana; they settled in various parts of what is now known as the Gulf States. Some of them made their homes in Biloxi, Ocean Springs, Pensacola, and New Orleans; and some moved on to Kentucky and Philadelphia. But many who settled on the Mississippi River a few miles above New Orleans (known as the German Coast) came from a group in Arkansas to whom John Law had given concessions. They fared badly there, and were making plans to return to their homes in Europe but Bienville persuaded them to remain, and gave them farms in the rich land along the river, mainly in what is now the parishes of St. Charles, and St. John the Baptist. This was a wilderness but the land was rich and game was plentiful. There was no drainage, and since there were no levees the settlers suffered from inundation as the river rose in the late spring. In every sense they suffered the travail of the pioneer: they had no plows, nor horses nor mules, nor oxen. Only a few had even a cow. Yet with hoe and spade, and some crude tools, these brave and industrious Germans built their homes, cleared the land, and produced crops to sustain them while they were in the process of establishing agricultural enterprises which were to make their community one of the most prosperous in the nation. Eventually they became eminent citizens, owning large sugar and rice plantations. In 1724 they built a small chapel on the right bank of the river, which in 1740 was replaced by a church, known today as the RED CHURCH, for it was painted red, and served as a landmark for boats on the Mississippi. It was here the word "DIXIE" was coined. The steamboats were accustomed to stop at Red Church Landing to pay off the hands before reaching New Orleans, and the men on the boat referred to the money as DIXIES, ten dollar notes which were widely circulated before the Civil War. The song "Dixie" was composed by Daniel Decatur Emmet in 1859 on a Sunday afternoon in response to a request for a "walk around" for a minstrel performance. It immediately became popular, and was published by a New Orleans publisher without permission. It should have brought Emmet a fortune. It is not known whether the publisher ever compensated him in any way. The first "Red Church" was burned in 1806, and was rebuilt. But in 1877 a demented Negro set fire to the priest's house, and all the valuable records were lost, for they were lodged in the rectory.

It cannot be said that all the German people who emigrated to this area were impoverished (although it would seem so from most accounts of them), for Deiler points out in his book on the German Coast that he learned from Penicaut that in 1719 the ship *Les Deux Freres* brought a number of Germans "with all sorts of merchandise and effects belonging to them," and they were apparently people of means who wanted to settle where they could find political and religious freedom.

Bayou des Allemands in St. Charles parish, about two miles from the river, is probably the first German village established in Louisiana, and it is now hardly any larger than when some twenty families first settled there.

Deiler says that Karl Friedrich D'Arensbourg, who was not in the employ of John Law, received a commission in 1721 to lead German immigrants to Louisiana, and to establish a new settlement. He had a land grant on the German Coast, and acted as judge and commander for the whole community; he was a German nobleman, and the Germans were more willing, therefore, to submit to his authority than to the authority of others who had attempted leadership.

Naturally in the course of time these German people married into French families, and many moved to New Orleans. But after two hundred and fifty years the family names of the first settlers are still predominant on the German Coast. Deiler mentions many in his book, *The Settlement of the German Coast of Louisiana*. Among them are:

George Rixner (Richner), who in 1839 married Amelie Perret. He had prospered, and set aside ten thousand dollars to build a house for her but she died before the house was built, and he used the money to build a magnificent tomb. They had one child, a daughter, who married an Italian, Count de Sarsana. She died in Marsala, Italy, and left a son, Ignatio.

The records of St. John the Baptist Church show the marriage of Anton Manz (now Montz), the son of Joseph Montz, and Anna Maria Raeser, of St. John. The Raeser family came to Louisiana in 1721. The Montz family is still in St. Charles parish, at LaPlace.

The descendants of the Waguespack family (originally Wagensbach — and later spelled eighteen different ways) are still on the German Coast, and eighty-four families of that name are living in New Orleans today (1969).

There are instances in which German names were changed into French. One in particular (often mentioned by historians) is that of Jean Zweig, who came to Louisiana on the ship *Les Deux Freres* in 1721. When his son married Suzanna Marchand, the French notary, having difficulty in pronouncing the groom's name asked its meaning, and being told that it meant "branch," he recorded the name as LaBranche. Then all Louisiana descendants of Jean Zweig were called Labranche or La Branche.

The name Wiltz was formerly 'Wilsz." Theodore von Wilsz, a native of Eisenach, Thuringia, married Christine Francken. Two of their sons came to America. One settled in Mobile, Alabama. The other, Joan Ludwig, born in 1711, settled in New Orleans. Before coming to Louisiana he married one of the Ziriac family of Saxony. After her death (in New Orleans) he married Marie Dolc, a native of Franckendel, Saxony. (It was Joan Ludwig who changed the name to **Wiltz,** dropping the title of Baron von Wilsz. (It is not known why, for they are said to have borne this title quite worthily.) By this marriage to Dolc, he had a daughter Louise Helene, who married a Langlois; another daughter Margaret who married (2) Jacinto Panis, and (1) Joseph Milhet. Their daughter M. Margarita Milhet married Don Pedro Georges Rousseau (father of Commodore Lawrence Rousseau, Gen. Gustave Sebastian Rousseau and others). The brother of Jon Ludwig Wiltz (who went to Mobile to live) married Suzanna Zweig (or La Branche). Their son, Jean Laurent Wiltz married Maria Colomb. Jean Baptiste Wiltz (whose portrait is in the Cabildo) was their son, who married (1) Suzanna Langlich, and (2) Marie Josepha Bahy.

From Jean Baptiste's marriage to Langliche there was a son, Leonard (portrait in the Cabildo), who married Marie Piquery (portrait in the Cabildo). From this marriage Leonard had a daughter Anne, who married her cousin, Edmond Valcour Wiltz, and a son Evariste Wiltz, who married Adelaide Montreuil.

From the marriage of Jean Baptiste to Marie Josepha Bahy, there was a son, Wisin, who married Louise Collier.

Among other early German settlers whose descendants are today prominent in Louisiana is Michael Zehringer (now Zeringue). He was from Franconia, Bavaria, and arrived here on the ship *Le Dromadaire* in 1720, with sixty workmen under the command of de la Tour, who was the chief engineer for the colony. He was an expert carpenter. After arriving he married Ursula Spaet, and they had a daughter

Salome. His wife and daughter both died in 1721. In the next year he married Barbara Haertel. By her he had four sons: Michael, Pierre Laurent, Joseph, and Jean Louis. The census of 1731 shows that he was living in New Orleans, and had sixteen Negro slaves, and twenty-seven cows. He died in 1738, and Louis Wiltz was a witness in his succession.

RIGHT BANK OF THE MISSISSIPPI
The German Village of Hoffen, 10 Lieues Above New Orleans November 12th, 1724

Simon Lambert is mentioned as "premier habitant et le plus haut sur le fleuve," the habitant living highest up on the right bank of the Mississippi. This location was on the upper side of Bonnet Carré Bend, about four miles below Edgard in the parish of St. John the Baptist. Lambert's habitation bears the number one. Thence the census enumerator proceeded down the right side of the river.

1. **Simon Lambert,** of Oberebesheim, diocese of Spire, Catholic; 40 years of age. His wife; and a son, 18 years of age. Five arpents cleared. Gave up his first place on account of inundation.

    1726: Six arpents cleared.

    1731: Occupants of this place, Jean Martin Lambert, son of the aforementioned, with wife and child.

    1764: Bartholomew Lambert, son of Jean Martin Lambert and Anna Eve Lambert, married Margarethe Troxler, daughter of Geo. T. and Marie Agnes Troxler.

2. **Conrad Friedrich,** of Rothenberg, diocese of Spire. (There is one Rothenberg east of Mannheim.) Catholic; 50 years old. His wife and three children. A daughter of 18 years; the youngest child five years old. Gave up first place on account of inundation. "A good worker".

    1726: Six arpents cleared.

    1726: Daughter Anna Barbara married Friedrich Markel from Wurtemberg, and, after whose death she married Nikolaus Wichner. Nikolaus Wichner and Anna Barbara Friedrich were the progenitors of most of the "Vicners", "Vicnaires" and "Vickners".

    1728: Daughter Anna Maria married Edw. Poupart, of Paris.

    1731: One child at home. Two negroes; one cow.

    About 1750 Sebastian Friedrich, son of Conrad Friedrich, married Regina Heidel (Haydel), daughter of Ambros Heidel, of St. John the Baptist. They lived below New Orleans.

3. **Johann Georg Troxler,** of Lichtenberg in Alsace. Catholic; 26 years old. A mason. His wife. "Fort bon travailleur". Two and one-half arpents cleared, on which he has been only since the beginning of the year having left the village in the rear. Exposed to inundation. Absent because of bad health. His wife is also sick. Lost his crop and his house. A neighbor, who cooked in a shed attached to Troxler's house, accidentally set fire to it.

    1731: Two children. Two negroes; one cow.

    Johann Georg Troxler was the progenitor of all the "Troxler" and "Trosclair" families in Louisiana.

4. **Johnn Georg Bock,** from the neighborhood of Fort Kehl in Baden. Catholic; 38 years old; weaver. His wife with child at the breast. One and a half arpents cleared. Two years on the place.

    1729: Marie Francoise, daughter of J. G. Bock and Cath. Hislinger, baptized.

    1731: Three children. One negro.

Now come to two tracts of land abandoned by Lambert and Friedrich.

5. **Wilhelm Ziriac,** also "Querjac", "Siriaque", and "Siriac", of Ilmenstadt, near Mayence. Formerly coachman to King Stanislaus. Catholic; 50 years old. His wife and daughter, seven years old. Two and a half arpents cleared. Two years on the place. "One of the more well to do people of the community. A good worker."

6. **Johann Callander,** of Aubrequin (Ober . . . ?), Palatinate. Catholic; 26 years old. His wife. A daughter. Sister-in-law; mother-in-law. One year on the place. Six arpents cleared, two and a half of which he bought from Peter Schmitz, and two and a half of which belonged to his mother-in-law and his children.

    1731: One child. One negro; one cow.

7. **Stephan Kiestenmacher,** of Cologne. Catholic; 39 years old. His wife and a daughter of 10 years. One and a half arpents cleared. Two years on the place. "Sick, broken down, miserable."

    1728: His daughter Margarethe married Louis Leonhard, from the Arkansas post.

    1731: Husband, wife and child. One **engage.** One negro; one cow.

8. **Jeremias Wagner,** of Orensburg (?) in the marquisate of Ansbach (Bavaria). Lutheran; 27 years of age. Hunter. His wife with a child at the breast. Sister-in-law. Two arpents cleared. One year on the place. "Very good man and a great hograiser".

    1726: Six arpents cleared.

9. **Leonhard Magdoff,** of Hermanse (?), Wurtemberg. Catholic; 45 years old. His wife. An adopted orphan boy, 10 years old. Two and a half arpents cleared. One year on the place. "A good worker. Has a very fine garden, is well lodged, and very prosperous in his affairs."

   1726: Six arpents cleared.
   1731: No children. Three cows.

10. **Andreas Schantz** (Chance), of Hochhausen, Franconia. Catholic; 25 years old. Miller. His wife with a child at the breast. Stepdaughter of 15 years. "A good man, well lodged." Has a cow from the company and a calf of eight days. A big hog and two little pigs.

    1726: Andreas Schantz married Maria Magdalena Gaffel, daughter of Leonhard G. and Cath. Wolf.
    1731: Two children. Four negroes; four cows.

11. **Johann Georg Betz,** of Weibstadt, diocese of Spire. Catholic; 32 years old. Butcher and **prevot.** His wife with a child at the breast. An orphan girl, nine years of age. Three arpents cleared. Three years on the place. A cow, a calf, and two pigs.

    1727: On the first of July, 1727, Betz, his wife, and two children are reported as inmates of the hospital in New Orleans, and on the 24th of August Betz died. His widow, who was a sister of Ambros Heidel (Haydel), then married Caspar Diehl of Alsace. The whole family, Diehl, his wife, two children, "a brother" (whose brother?) were murdered in 1729 by the Natchez Indians in the great massacre in Natchez.

12. **Johann Adam Matern,** of Rosenheim, in Upper Alsace. Catholic; 26 years old. Weaver. His wife with a child at the breast; two sisters-in-law, 18 and 20 years of age. One and a half year on the place. Two and half arpents cleared. "A good worker", who deserves some negroes. Three pigs.

    1731: Three children. Three negroes; seven cows.

13. **Caspar Dubs** (Toups) from the neighborhood of Zurich, Switzerland. Protestant; 40 years of age. Butcher and **prevot.** His wife; two boys, 10 and 12 years old. Two years on the place. One and half arpents cleared. Three pigs.

    1728: Caspar Dubs married Maria Barbara Kittler, from Wurtemberg.
    1731: Six arpents cleared.
    Caspar Dubs was the progenitor of all the Toups families in Louisiana.

14. **Ambros Heidel** (Haydel), of Neukirchen, electorate of Mayence. Catholic; 22 years old. Baker. His wife; his brother, 18 years old; his brother-in-law, aged 13, crippled. One and a half years on the place. "Good worker, very much at ease." One pig.

> Ambros Heidel's younger brother is mentioned for the last time in 1727. It is possible that he was murdered by the Natchez Indians with the family of his sister. See No. 11. From the entry there it does not appear whether the brother murdered was the husband's or the wife's brother.
>
> 1731: Ambros Heidel, wife, two children. One **engage**. Three negroes and two cows.

15. **Jacob Ritter,** of Lustuen in Wurtemberg (Lustnau near Tubingen?). Catholic; 28 years old. Shoemaker. His wife. One and half arpents cleared. Six months on the place. One pig.

> 1726: Four arpents cleared.
>
> 1731: Two cows.

16. **Michael Vogel,** of Altdorf, Suevia, Germany. Catholic; 40 years old. Cooper. A little hard of hearing. Son of two years, daughter of eleven years in New Orleans. Sixteen verges cleared. (Ten verges = one arpent.) Two years on the place. One pig.

> 1726: Four arpents cleared.
>
> 1726: Margarethe Vogel, his daughter, married Jean Bossier, farmer from Natchitoches.
>
> 1731: Two children. One negro; two cows.

17. **Sebastian Funck,** of Hagenau, Alsace. Catholic; 30 years old. His wife. Child of one year; orphan girl of 16 years. Two years on the place. Five arpents cleared, which he bought from two Germans, of whom one went to Natchitoches, while the other took land from Governor Bienville near New Orleans, which he has now held two years. One pig.

> 1726: Husband, wife, two children. Four arpents cleared.

18. **Michael Horn,** of Limbal, near Mayence. Catholic; 39 years old. His wife and a daughter of eight years. Fifteen verges cleared. Fifteen days on the place. Came from "the old village". His sickness prevents him from succeeding. Michael Horn's daughter married Louis Toups.

> 1726: Four arpents cleared.

19. A strip of land of eight verges for the surgeon of the community. A hut on it. Abandoned.

Here ends the village of Hoffen, and the census man now leaves the river front and proceeds to the two old villages in the rear, which were mentioned before.

Old German Village (i.e., the "second" one. See before.). Three-fourths of a mile from the Mississippi.

20. **Balthasar Monthe,** of Troppau, in Silesia, Germany. Catholic; 42 years old. His wife. Daughter of 13 months. One and a fifth arpents cleared. Three years on the place. "A good worker. Everything well arranged on his place. Was sick the whole summer." Two pigs. He died in 1727.

21. **Johann Georg Raeser,** of Biebrich, in the electorate of Mayence. Catholic; 32 years old. Blacksmith. His wife. An orphan girl of 18 years. Two arpents cleared. Three years on the place. "Well arranged. Good worker."

    1726: Husband, wife, three children, brother-in-law. Six arpents cleared. One pig.

    1731: Husband, wife, one child.

22. **Johann Jacob Bebloquet** (?) of Lamberloch, Alsace. Lutheran; 36 years old. Hunter. His wife. Three children, two boys and one girl, ranging from two to thirteen years of age. One and a half arpents cleared. Three years on the place. Two pigs. "Well arranged. Good worker."

23. **Johann Cretzmann** (Kretzmann), of canton Berne, Switzerland. Calvinist; 46 years old. His wife; son of five years. One and a half arpents cleared. "His affairs well regulated. Demands his passage." Did not get it.

24. **Balthasar Marx,** of Wullenberg, Palatinate (one Wollenberg near Wimpfen), Catholic; 27 years old. Nailsmith. His wife, 22 years old. "His wife had a miscarriage last year on account of working at the pounding trough ('pilon'). He went to New Orleans to get some salt and had to give a barrel of shelled rice for three pounds. His affairs excellently arranged. Good worker." One and a half arpents cleared. Three years on the place.

    1731: Husband, wife, two children. One **engage.** One negro; three cows.

    1775: **Jean Simon Marx,** son of Balthasar and Marianne Aglae Marx, married Cath. Troxler, daughter of Nik. T. and Cath. Matern (St. James parish).

25. **Bernard Wich,** of Tainlach, in Wurtemberg. Lutheran; 46 years old. His wife. Three children, a boy and two girls, from 13 years down to two months. Two arpents cleared. A pig.

    1731: Two children. One **engage.** One negro.

26. **Johann Rommel** (now Rome), of Kinhart, Palatinate. Catholic; 24 years of age. Tailor. His wife. One and a half arpents cleared. Three years on the place. A pig.

    1728: Jean Rommel baptized.

    1731: Three children. Two cows.

27. **Catharine Weller** (ine), 49 years old, from Heilbronn, Wurtemberg, widow of August Paul, a Lutheran, a tailor. "Expects a child. Alone and poor. Has no provisions and needs some assistance. Six verges cleared."

28. **Anna Kuhn,** widow of Johann Adam Zweig (Labranche). Her husband was a Catholic, and died in Biloxi. Daughter of twelve years. One and a half arpents cleared. "Has no provisions and no seed for the next year. Needs some assistance."

    1729: Daughter Anna Margarethe Zweig married Pierre Bridel, a soldier, and a native of Bretagne. According to the marriage entry the bride was born in Bollweiler, Alsace.

29. **Magdalena Fromberger,** 50 years old. Catholic; widow of George Meyer from Ingitippil (?), Suevia, Germany. "Her son, Nik. Mayer, is crippled but industrious in the cooper trade. He also makes galoches which are a great help when shoes are scarce. An orphan girl, 20 years old. One and a half arpents cleared. Three years on the place. A pig.

    1731: Nik. Meyer. His wife and a child. One **engage**.

    Two negroes; two cows.

30. **Margarethe Reynard** (Reinhard?), from Bauerbach, Baden. Catholic; 46 years old. Separated from Johann Leuck (?), who lives on the Mississippi. Daughter from first marriage, aged seven years. Seven verges cleared. Three years on the place.

31. **Catherine Hencke,** of Horenburg, Brandenburg, widow of Christian Grabert, a Catholic, who died in Biloxi, aged 50 years. A daughter, 14 years old. Both sick. She needs some assistance and is very willing to work. Two arpents cleared.

32. **Christian Grabert,** Grabert, of Brandenburg. Catholic; 23 years old. His wife. An orphan child, 13 years old. Two arpents cleared. Three years on the place. One pig.

    1726: Christian Grabert, his wife, mother-in-law, sister-in-law, and sister. Six arpents cleared.

33. **Phillipp Zahn,** of Grosshoeffein, Hungary. Catholic; 25 years of age. His wife. Three arpents cleared. Two years on the place. A pig.

    1726: One child. Four arpents cleared.

1727: As widower of Margarethe Wiethen (ine) Philipp Zahn married in this year Marie Schlotterbecker of Wurtemberg, widow of Jacob Stalle and sister of the wife of Thomas Lesch.

The census at this time mentions the land forming the passage of three arpents' width, leading from the river front to the concession of M. de Meure. According to a map of 1731, this place was about two miles above Hahnville.

34. **Johann Jacob Foltz** (now "Folse") of Ramstein, Palatinate. Catholic; 26 years old. Shoemaker. His wife. A child of one year. Four arpents cleared. Two years on the place. One pig. This year made only seven barrels of rice on account of inundation. Was sick the whole summer.

   1731: Two children. Two cows.

35. **Bernhard Anton,** of Schweigen, in Wurtemberg. Lutheran; 30 years old. His wife. A boy, 10 years old. About four arpents cleared. Two pigs. Two years on the place. Made this year 20 barrels of rice, and would have also made 60 barrels of corn, if there had been no inundation. "Good worker."

   1731: Three children. One **engage.** Six cows.

After enumerating these families, the census of 1724 continues:

"All these German families enumerated in the present census raise large quantities of beans and mallows, and do much gardening, which adds to their provisions and enables them to fatten their animals, of which they raise many. They also work to build levees in front of their places.

"If all these small farmers were in the neighborhood of New Orleans they could raise vegetables and poultry. They could make their living well and add to the ornament of the town, as their small frontage on the river brings their houses with the gardens behind them so close together that they look like villages. But this agreeable condition unfortunately does not exist in New Orleans, owing to the greed for land of those who demanded large concessions, not with the intention of cultivating them, but only of reselling them.

"If these German families, the survivors of a great number who have been here, are not assisted by negroes, they will gradually perish; for what can a man and his wife accomplish on a piece of land, when, instead of resting themselves and taking their meals after their hard work, they must go to the pounding trough **(pilon)** to prepare their food, a very toilsome work, the consequences of which are dangerous for men and women. Many receive injuries, and many women get seriously hurt. When one of the two falls sick, it is absolutely necessary that the other should do all the work alone, and thus both perish, examples of which are not rare.

"The ground is so hard in the lower part of the colony that one must always have the hoe ready, and the weeds come out so strong and so quickly, that it seems after a short while as if no work had been done at all. The land is covered with dead trees and stumps, and these people have no draught animals (as this census shows there was not a single horse on the German Coast, and of the 56 families only six had cows), they cannot use the plow, but must always work with the pickaxe and the hoe.

"This together with the hard work on the pilon, causes these poor people to perish, who are good workers and willing, and who do not desire anything more than to remain in a country where they are free from burdensome taxation and from the rule of the master of their land — a lot quite different from that of the peasants in Germany.

"They would consider themselves very happy to get one or two negroes, according to the land they have, and we would soon find them to be good overseers. The only thing to be done would be to visit them once or twice a year, to see what use they are making of them, and to take the negroes away from the lazy ones and give them to the industrious. But this would hardly be necessary, as these people are by nature industrious and more contented than the French.

"They could also feed their negroes very well on account of the great quantities of vegetables they raise. They could also sell a great deal to the large planters, and these, assured of a regular supply, could give more attention to the raising of indigo, the cutting of timber, and to other things suitable for exportation to France and Cape Frances (San Domingo). I am persuaded that a great timber trade could be established with the West Indian Islands, where timber is getting scarcer and is dear."

LEFT BANK OF THE MISSISSIPPI RIVER
Continuation of the Census of 1724

The land immediately above New Orleans and on the same side of the Mississippi, beginning beyond the moat of the upper town limit (now foot of Bienville street), and extending up to the center of the great bend of the river at Southport, beyond Carrollton, belonged to M. Bienville — in all, 213½ arpents river front.

This is, no doubt, the land which the census enumerator, a French official, quoted above, had in view when he said, "If these German farmers were in the neighborhood of New

Orleans * * * ." And when he speaks of "the greed of those who demanded large concessions," he evidently referred also to Governor Bienville.

The lower portion of Bienville's land—from Bienville street to somewhere about Felicity road, 58½ arpents' front—Bienville reserved for his own habitation. Of this tract he sold a part to the Jesuit fathers. From Felicity road up to southport he placed, as has been stated, twelve German and a few French families, most of whom received their titles on and after the first of January, 1723. But by the time the census of 1724 was taken, a number of these had left. The fact that the Germans had already once before lost their all by a great hurricane and inundation, and the failure of Bienville to build a levee, although he had guaranteed one to them in their titles, and the consequent inundations they were subjected to even in the first year, together with the exacting conditions of rental to be fulfilled — all these were causes to compel these people to sell out their contracts as quickly as they could. Some had already left during the first year, and Jacob Huber, the last German to remain on Bienville's land, stayed only from 1723 to 1727.

Partly from census reports, and partly from chains of titles of Bienville's hands, the author has been able to ascertain the names of most of the German storm victims who settled on Bienville's lands:

Peter Bayer, from Wankenloch, near Durlach, Baden, who had taken six arpents of Bienville's land above New Orleans.

Caspar Hegli, a Swiss, from near Lucerne. "Six arpents. Catholic; 35 years old. His wife. A daughter. Two orphan boys. A cow, a heifer, a young bull, and three pigs. Two years on the place. Used two and a half barrels of seed rice and did not make more than three barrels on account of inundation. Has a very fine garden enclosed by palisades. He has made a good levee and is a good worker. He deserves a negro." (Census of 1724.)

Jacob Huber, with six arpents. "Native of Suevia, Germany. Catholic: 45 years old. His wife, son of 16 years. One **engage.** One cow, one heifer, a pig. Made no crop on account of inundation. Good worker." (Census of 1724.)

    Jacob Huber's son Christoph married Marie Josephine St. Ives. Descendants write the name now "Oubre", "Ouvre", "Hoover".

Andreas Krestmann, or Christmann, from Augsburg, with his two sons, 10 and 12 years old. Six arpents. "Wheelwright. His wife. Two orphan girls, eight and fifteen years old. Two years on the place. A cow, a heifer, a calf and three pigs. He is industrious and is at work fencing in his cleared land. He made a good levee and paid in advance the workmen who made it for him at a cost of 100 pistoles. Deserves a negro."

These four men occupied a portion of Bienville's land from the present First street of New Orleans to Napoleon avenue. Further up, beginning about the upper line of Audubon Park, were:

Simon Kuhn, of Weissenburg, Ansbach, Bavaria. "His wife, daughter, son-in-law, Daniel Hopf, 20 years of age of Cassen, diocese of Spire. Orphan boy 12 years old. Cow, calf, three pigs. One year on the land. Had to change his engagements twice, having been forced to give up his cabin on account of water. Good worker." (Census of 1724.) An elder daughter of Simon Kuhn, Anna Kuhn, was the widow of Johann Adam Zweig (Labranche, who had died in Biloxi). She had a daughter of the age of 12 years. The orphan boy, 12 years old, was, no doubt a relative, and very likely that Jean Labranche who, in 1737, married Susanna Marchand and became the progenitor of all the Labranche families in Louisiana. Daniel Hopf (French spelling "Yopf" and "Poff") married, in 1727, Anna Maria Werich, of Lampaitz, German Lorraine. A daughter of this second marriage, Renée "Poff", married, 1752, in Pointe Coupée, Pierre Baron.

Thomas Lesch (now "Leche" and "Laiche"), with three arpents. "His wife. One **engage.**" (Census of 1726.) Thomas Lesch married, in 1725, in the cathedral of New Orleans, Anna Schoderbecker of Wurtemberg. Only daughters were born from this marriage:

> **Margarethe Lesch** married one Peter Engel, a carpenter, whose name occurs also in the spelling "Aingle", "Ingle", "Hingle", and "Engle". There were three sons, Simon Sylvestre and Santiago Hingle, who married into the Bura family in Plaquemines parish (Bura's Settlement). The "Hingle" family is quite numerous there.
>
> **Regina Lesch,** another daughter of Thomas Lesch, married one Christian Philippson.

In matters of descent not the language but the **blood** is the vital matter, and the blood alone. We must therefore classify the Louisiana Creoles according to the blood of their progenitors, and say:

There are

Creoles of French descent,

Creoles of German descent,

Creoles of Spanish descent,

and still others, for instance Creoles of Irish descent (the McCarty family) and Creoles of Scotch descent (the Pollock family).

WHAT IS THE PROBABLE NUMBER OF THE CREOLES OF GERMAN DESCENT?

This question may be answered in the words of the promise, given to Abraham: they are as numerous "as the sands on the sea shore."

The church registers of St. John the Baptist prove that the German pioneers were blessed with enormously large families. It seems that heaven wanted to compensate them in this manner for the many dear ones they had lost in the ports of France, on the high seas, in Biloxi, and during the first period of their settling in Louisiana. I found fourteen of them, sixteen, eighteen, and once even twenty-two children in a family.

Yet, in spite of this great number of children there was no difficulty in providing for the numerous daughters. There was a great scarcity of women in Louisiana in early times. Indeed, as we have seen, prostitutes were gathered in Paris and sent to Louisiana to provide wives for the colonists. Few of these lewd women ever had any children, and their families became extinct in the second and third generation. See census of 1721 where it is stated that fourteen soldiers were married but that there was not a single child in these fourteen families.

According to this census — when the Germans on the German Coast and those on the Arkansas River were not enumerated — there were only thirty women with 21 children for every hundred white men in the district of New Orleans. No wonder that the young Frenchmen, especially those of the better class, chose wives from among the German maidens, who were not only morally and physically sound and strong, but had also been reared by their German mothers to be good house-wives.

Of the Heidel (Haydel) family, whose descendants are so numerous that one of them told the writer: "My family alone can populate a whole parish (county) in Louisiana," female descendants of the first five generations married into seventy-four different French families, and it very seldom happened that there was but one marriage between two families. Remember that in these statistics are still wanting the entries of the many registers that were burned at the "Red Church" and those of the volumes burned with the cathedral of New Orleans in 1788.

Yes, even into the most exclusive circles, into the families of the officials and of the richest merchants the German girls married, they became the wives of French and Spanish officers of ancient nobility in whose descendants German blood still flows.

Only one example: female descendants of Karl Friedrich D'Arensbourg married into the families of de la Chaise, de la Tour, de la Grue, de Villeré, de L'Home, de Vaugine, d'Olhond, Laland d'Apremont, de Bosclair, de Livaudais, de Blanc, de la Barre, de Léry, de la Vergne, de Buys, Forstall, Trudeau, Perret, St. Martin, Montegut, Lanaux, Beauregard, Bouligny, Suzeneau, le Breton, Tricou, Duverjé, Urquhart, de Reggio, Rathbone, Durel, Luminais, Bermudez.

When General O'Reilly, in the year 1769, forced the Spanish yoke upon Louisiana, he selected six of the most prominent citizens, whom he had shot in order to intimidate the hostile population. Of these six "martyrs of Louisiana," were not fewer than three who had wives from German families:

Joseph Milhet, the richest merchant of the colony, had as his wife Margarethe Wiltz, whose father was from Eisenach, in Thuringia, while her mother was born in Frankenthal, Saxony;

Marquis, the commander-in-chief of the insurgents, was married to a daughter of an Alsatian officer, Gregor Volant, from Landsee, near Strassburg, and

Joseph de Villere, under whose command the Germans of the German Coast had marched against the Spanish in 1768, had a grandchild of Karl Friedrich D'Arensbourg as his wife.

THE GERMAN LANGUAGE AMONG THE CREOLES OF LOUISIANA

As a rule, the German girls took German husbands, and whole families married into one another. To give but one example, it may be mentioned here that out of the ten children of one Jacob Troxler not fewer than eight married into the Heidel (Haydel) family. In such families the German language survived longest, and old Creoles of German descent have told me that their grandparents still understood and were able to speak the German language, although they were not able to read and write it, as there were never any German teachers on the German coast. Among the old records is a building contract of 1763 written in German, in which one Andreas Bluemler, a carpenter, obligated himself to build "for 2000 livres and a cow, a heifer and a black calf," a house for Simon Traeger (Tregre). A law-suit followed and so this building contract, together with the court records of the case, were preserved to the present day.

In consequence, however, of the many family ties between the Germans and the French, and in consequence of the custom of the Creoles to marry into related families, French gradually became the family language even in those German families which had preserved the German language during three generations.

Some few German words, however, can occasionally be heard even yet in the Creole families of German descent, especially words relating to favorite dishes, "which our grandmother was still able to cook, but which are no longer known in our families."

German names of persons, too, have been preserved, although in such a mutilated form that they can hardly be recognized. Thus the tradition in the Heidel (Haydel) family is that the first Heidel born in Louisiana was called "Anscopp," with the French nasal pronunciation of the first syllable. I could not get the original German for "Anscopp" until I compiled the genealogy of the family when I found that the first Heidel born in Louisiana was christened "Jean Jacques." Now I knew that they called him in the family "Hans Jacob," and that by throwing out the initial "h" and contracting "Hans Jacob" the name was changed into "Anscopp." In a similar manner "Hans Peter" was changed into "Ampete" and "Hans Adam" in to "Ansdam."

The German language disappeared quickest in families where a German had married a French girl. There no German was spoken at all, and even the Christian names customary in German families disappeared even as early as in the second generation, as now also the French wife and her relatives had to be considered in the giving of names to the children. Instead of Hans Peter, Hans Jacob, Michl, Andre, and Matthis, the boys of the German farmers were now called: Sylvain, Honoré, Achille, Anatole, Valcourt, Lezin, Ursin, Marcel, Symphorion, Homer, Ovide, Onésiphore and Onesime; and instead of the good old German names Anna Marie, Marianne, Barbara, Katharine, Veronika, and Ursula, the German girls were called: Hortense, Corinne, Elodie, Euphémie, Félicité, Melicerte, Désiré, Pélagie, Constance, Pamela; and after the French revolution each family had her "Marie Antoinette."

THE FATE OF THE GERMAN FAMILY NAMES
AMONG THE CREOLES

The changes which the German family names underwent among the Creoles are most regrettable. Without exception, all names of the first German colonists of Louisiana were changed, and most of the Creoles of German descent at the present time no longer know how the names of their German ancestors looked. Sometimes they were changed beyond recognition, and only by tracing some thirty families with all their branches through all the church records still available; by going through eighty boxes of official documents in the keeping of the "Louisiana Historical Society;" by ransacking the archives of the city of New Orleans and of a number of country parishes, and by compiling the genealogies of these families has the author been able to recognize the German people of the different generations, to ascertain their original names, and to connect the old German settlers with the generation of the Creoles of German descent now living.

Various circumstances contributed to the changing of these names. The principal one was, no doubt, the fact that some of the old German colonists were not able to write their names. Their youth had fallen into the period of the first fifty years after the "Thirty Years' War" and into the last years of the war when the armies of Louis XIV of France devastated the Palatinate. In consequence of the general destruction and the widespread misery of that period, schools could hardly exist in their homes. It was therefore not the fault of these people if they could not read and write their names. Moreover, as the parents could not tell their children in Louisiana how to write their names, these children had to accept what French and Spanish teachers and priests told them, and what they found in official documents. But French and Spanish officials and priests heard the German names through French and Spanish ears, and wrote them down as they thought these sounds should be written in French or Spanish. Moreover, Spanish and French officials and priests at that early time were not great experts in the grammar of their own language.

Finally, the early German colonists did not pronounce their own names correctly, but according to their home dialect.

To prove the last assertion three German names shall be considered: **"Schaf," "Schoen," "Manz."** In South Germany, where most of these people came from, "a" is pronounced broad, and almost approaches the "o." The South German peasant does not say "meine Schafe," but "mei' Schof." No wonder that the French officials spelled the name "Schaf" "Chauffe." In this form the name still exists in Louisiana.

"Schoen" was evidently pronounced like German "Schehn," for which reason the French spelled it "Chesne," "Chaigne," and "Chin."

And the name "Manz" for the same reason was changed into "Montz."

Many changes in the spelling of the German names follow the general "Law of the mutation of Consonants," called Grimm's Law, which may be roughly stated thus: "Consonants uttered by the same organ of speech are frequently interchanged."

NOTES: (from Deiler's book)

There was a German settlement at Pascagoula, the founding date of which is not known, but Deiler says that Ross, an English ship captain, found there a cotton crop and a cotton gin in 1772 on Krebs' farm. The last will and testament of Krebs, written in New Orleans in Spanish, 1776, gives his full name as Hugo Ernestus Krebs. He was from Neumagen on the Moselle, Germany, and left fourteen grown children, whose descendants still own the Krebs farm. It is situated on Krebs Lake. The farm house was still standing in 1906, when it was well over 175 years old. The heavy cypress lumber was still in excellent condition. In fact, the whole house was in good condition, and habitable.
Krebs married Marie Simon de la Pointe.

When Law became a bankrupt the Germans on the Arkansas River and at English Turn were left stranded when they needed assistance. They had not yet been able to build their houses and clear the land to produce crops. And Law's agent, Levens, refused to transfer the business of the company. They were compelled to ask help of their only friends, the Arkansas and the Sothui Indians. Finally help from this source failed, and small-pox broke out among both the Germans and the Indians. They were forced to give up all and abandon the concession. Only forty-seven remained, whom La Harpe met there on the 20th of March 1722, when he installed Dudemaine Dufresne as agent. But when La Harpe returned sometime later he found that these too had left and, it is supposed, moved to New Orleans, where there were then only three of four houses and a number of huts.

Also Christian names as well as the names of places (see Ettler, from Colmar) and nicknames became family names.

The daughter of one Jacob Helfer was entered into the marriage register as "Mademoiselle Yocle," because her father was called familiarly "Jockel," which is a nickname for Jacob.

The family of Thomas Lesch was for some time lost to me until I recovered it under the name of "Daumas"="Thomas."

Remarkable was the fate of the name "Hofmann." The forms Ofman, Aufman, Eaufman, Haufman, Ophman, Oghman, Ocman, Hochman, Haukman, Hacmin, Aupemane, Augman, Olphman, and Ocmane were not the only changes that occurred. The family came from Baden and thus "de Bade" was often added to the name. In course of time the people forgot the meaning of "de Bade," and a new name was formed, "Badeau," with a feminine form, "Badeauine."

The eldest daughter of one Hofmann married a man by the name of "Achtziger." This name seems to have given a great deal of trouble. I found "Hacksiger," "Chactziger," "Oxtiger," "Oxtixer," "Axtigre," "Harzstingre," "Astringer," "Haxsitper," and "Horticair," but early the French officials (like in the case "Zweig-Labranche") translated the name Achtziger into French "Quatrevingt," to which they were in the habit of adding the original name as best they knew how. Now, as the eldest daughter of this Hofmann was called "Madame Quatrevingt," they seem to have called her younger sister in a joking way "Mademoiselle Quarante," for when she married she appears in the church register as "Mademoiselle Quarantine," alias "Hocman."

Finally, another name shall be mentioned here, which is now pronounced "Sheckshnyder." The legend is that six brothers by the name of "Schneider" came across the sea, and each one of them was called "one of the six Schneiders," hence the name "Sheckshnyder;" but this legend is, like many another legend, false. The first priest of St. John the Baptist, the German Capuchin father Bernhard von Limbach (1772), who wrote even the most difficult German names phonetically correct, entered the name as "Scheckschneider," which is an old German name. The progenitor of this family, Hans Reinhard Scheckschneider, is mentioned on the passenger list of one of the four pest ships which sailed from L'Orient on the twenty-fourth of January, 1721. There were no "six Schneiders" on board, only he, his wife and two sons, one of whom died in Brest. Yet he was already called "Chezneider," even on board ship.

A NOTE ON BIENVILLE'S WEALTH

Jean Baptiste Le Moyne Sieur de Bienville finally retired and went to Paris to spend the remaining years of his life. When Jean Milhet went to France for the purpose of appealing to the king to let Louisiana remain a French province, he was Bienville's guest for nearly three years, and found him in very comfortable circumstances. Milhet was then the richest man in Louisiana. All historians refer to his great wealth but do not explain what his holdings were or how he acquired them, whether by land grants or by trading, or by both, which is very likely. But the manner in which Bienville acquired his wealth is clearly set forth by Deiler. It is of record that Bienville acquired by a grant all the land from the upperside of Bienville Street to the present Southport, and from the Mississippi back to the present Claiborne Avenue. Thus 213 arpents of river front belonged to him. After selecting the site for the future city of New Orleans in 1718, he hastened to procure as much as possible of the best land adjacent to the city. He got a second grant of 112 arpents front on the west side of the river below Algiers, beginning at what is now Vallette Street and extending down the river.

Deiler says that after these two grants had been made by the Superior Council of Louisiana on the 21st of March, 1719, a royal edict was issued on November 7, 1719, forbidding governors, lieutenant governors, and intendants to own plantations. They were permitted to have vegetable gardens only. But Bienville, who had already received Horn Island "in socage tenure," had these two large new grants approved by the directors in Paris. Indeed he did not let any grass grow under his feet! In order to obey the letter, if not the spirit, of the Royal edict, says Deiler, Bienville now designated $53\frac{1}{2}$ out of $213\frac{1}{2}$ arpents immediately above New Orleans as his habitation, "the vegetable garden," which he extended from Bienville Street to Felicity Road, and from the Mississippi to Claiborne Avenue, comprising more than the present city of New Orleans.

Not yet satisfied, Bienville established a second "vegetable garden" by taking forty-nine arpents from a depth of eighty arpents of his grant on the west side of the river, and designating it also as his habitation. As he was prohibited from working the remainder of his two large grants (outside of his habitation and vegetable garden) he introduced a system of "feudal tenure," and sold to people for high annual ground rent, to be paid in money and/or products, or in manual labor. Among the first entering into such a deal were twelve German families. But they soon grew tired of working mainly for the benefit of the "Father of the Colony," and moved on to the German Coast.

In 1722 Bienville established himself on his land composed of the square bounded by Bienville, Iberville, Decatur and Chartres Streets. The square adjacent, bounded by Bienville, Iberville, Chartres and Royal Streets, he sold to the Jesuits in 1726, with other land that he owned. In 1728 the Jesuits purchased another five arpents from him, and gradually acquired the whole section up to Felicity Street. The original Jesuits' plantation, therefore, began on Bienville Street.

Although Bienville acquired some wealth, it cannot be denied that he was entitled to more than France ever could or would pay him for establishing a colony and founding a city which was to become one of the world's great centers of commerce, industry, science and art. While all the land he held, with or even without its buildings may be worth hundreds of millions today, had he sold it in his time, the proceeds probably would have been scarcely enough to buy today a first class automobile, which any modern-day clerk or salesman can own. Considering his services to the king and to the people of the colony, he would have been a dunce not to acquire a good quantity of land.

Among Landmarks of New Orleans
The Building of the Customhouse

The huge granite building on Canal Street, occupying the entire block between North Peters and Decatur Streets, is the United States Customhouse. On or near this spot the Spanish Governor Miró had erected a pretentious edifice for the government after the fire of 1788, which nearly destroyed the city. But in 1794 Carondelet demolished this structure and others close by to build Fort St. Louis, which covered the block. After the Louisiana Purchase the fort was demolished, and in the middle of the block a brick building of moderate size was erected to be used as a United States Customhouse. Along side of this building stood a bethel. By 1848 the commerce of the city had increased to so great an extent that the government found it necessary to build a larger customhouse, and this site was selected for the building. The land (i.e., the whole block) was ceded to the United States Government by the First Municipality on June 29, 1848, and the construction of the building began shortly thereafter. But it was many years before this building was completed. Henry Clay laid the cornerstone. By 1860 the walls had been built up to the architrave line of the intablature, and all the floorbeams of the fourth story were in place. A temporary roof had been placed on the building, making it habitable. But the work was stopped at the outbreak of the Civil War, and was not resumed until 1871, when it continued under the supervising architect of the United States Treasury. But progress was still as slow as ever. Nobody seemed to care whether the building was ever finished. The second story was entirely finished and ready for occupancy in 1879, and the third story was finished in 1881. The fourth story was not entirely completed until 1913.

The foundation of this building is remarkable. It rests upon a plank flooring seven feet below the sidewalk, upon which is a grillage of twelve inch logs covered by a layer of concrete a foot deep, concrete also being used to fill the spaces between the logs. The tradition that bales of cotton were used in the foundation is not true. As expected, the building settled as much as two and a half feet. But it settled evenly and with no damage. The laying of the foundation for so heavy a building on soggy soil without piling required considerable skill and good engineering. This is today a magnificent building. It was once considered the finest building in America. The staircase is of marble, being double up to the second story, and then the full width of the hall to the next floor. The stairs to the third floor are of iron. The ceiling is of ground glass, with a stained glass border, supported by fourteen marble columns, the capital of each of which is

The Custom House — New Orleans

embellished with reliefs of Juno and Mercury. The cost of these columns was $23,000 each.

Although not completely finished, in 1862 and 1863 the building was used as a prison for Confederate officers taken in the siege of Port Hudson.

The building was finally completed in 1883, thirty-five years after construction began. (Except the fourth story which was not entirely completed until 1913.)

The technical superintendence (at the beginning) was under P.G.T. Beauregard, then Major of Engineers (U.S. Army). But during the long period of construction there were other architects engaged in the work. The original plans were drawn by A. T. Wood, and construction actually began in 1848. But after the ground floor was well under way, a delegation of army engineers was sent from Washington to inspect the building. It was found that the original plan called for rooms without proper lighting or ventilation, which was unsatisfactory. Colonel James Harrison Dakin, who was then engaged in constructing the (old) capitol house at Baton Rouge, was given the commission as architect and superintendent of construction. He revised Wood's plans, and created a beautiful Grecian rotunda in the center of the building, and placed the rooms on the outside. He also substituted cast iron columns for the heavy groined vaulting as planned by Wood.

Mr. Dakin resigned in September of 1851, but the work continued according to his revised plan. There had been differences of opinion among the supervisors concerning the work, and Mr. Dakin said that he could not discharge his duties with proper fervor and interest, and that was his reason for resigning. A. T. Wood remained on the job; and James Gallier (March, 1851) was appointed Acting Architect. One reason, among others, for the slow progress in the construction was that the granite for the building came from

Quincy, Massachusetts, and shipments reached New Orleans only every few months. Even unloading the huge blocks was a long and tedious job. But A. C. Jones constructed a "steam stevedore," which was shaped like a locomotive and moved without rails. It handled the granite blocks ten times faster than labor could.

In November of 1851, Lewis E. Reynolds, a noted architect of New Orleans, and author of the COMPRESSIBILITY AND MOTION OF THE SOIL OF NEW ORLEANS, was appointed Acting Architect by Washington, with orders to keep the work going. Also A. T. Wood was instructed to see that the work continued according to his original drawings, which was a blunder on the part of Washington, for both Dakin and Gallier had already changed the plans, and the changes had been approved. It was quite natural that friction would come between Reynolds and Wood, and it did. At one point Wood demanded that he be provided a private room in the architects' office, and this Reynolds refused to allow. Finally, in the interest of peace, and so as not to impede the work, which was progressing slowly enough, Reynolds had a private room prepared for Wood. The matter of the private room was not the only cause of disagreement between Reynolds and Wood. Reynolds claimed, for instance, that Wood ordered bricks for the building to be shipped from other places, and as shipments were often long delayed the work lagged. He stated that bricks made in New Orleans were as good as any made in the north or anywhere else. He stated that the "strongest bricks in the United States can be made at our door."

At this time (April of 1852) the Commissioners for the customhouse were: Samuel J. Peters and George C. Lawrason, the latter having been appointed Collector of Customs, the post formerly occupied by S. J. Peters and William Freret. They urged Mr. Reynolds to speed up the work as much as possible, and he made a bold attempt to do so. But the incessant warfare among the architects and supervisors made progress difficult. The authorities in Washington were apparently displeased with the manner in which this construction was handled, for J. K. Wharton, who had been clerk of the original commissioners since November of 1848, was made Acting Architect pro tem on everything pertaining to the building of the customhouse.

Although some critics called the customhouse "a granite monstrosity," when it was completed, it is in fact a magnificent building, and can be considered one of the finest structures in America. And certainly it has served a useful purpose. It housed the United States Custom Offices, the Internal Revenue Department, the U.S. Engineers, the Sub-Treasury, the Lighthouse Inspectors, the Land Office, the Weather Bureau, and an observatory on the roof. The United States Postoffice in New Orleans, first established in 1803, and situated in the Merchants Exchange, was transferred in 1860 to the Customhouse, and was the main postoffice until the postoffice building was erected on Camp Street opposite Lafayette Square, when the Customhouse office became a branch. There have been many United States buildings erected since that time but the old Customhouse, though shunned in a way, stands as solid as ever. It can be said that the architects who had a hand in its planning and construction merit high praise, for they have erected an edifice which will stand for centuries.

1. In those days this block faced the levee. Since that time the Mississippi River has receded approximately four city blocks to the east and built up a batture, now of solid foundation on which stand many large buildings. The business houses in the vicinity of Front Street and the lower part of Canal Street stand where formerly ships lay at anchor.
2. Stuart O. Landry says, in Louisiana Almanac and Fact Book, this building was a **courthouse.**
3. The cost of the building was estimated to be $800,000, and it was to be entirely fire-proof; the walls of the vaulted rooms, according to specifications, were of great thickness, and only iron could be used in the construction of the floors. It is said that less wood was used in the whole structure than in any building of its size in the world.
4. The cost of the building, instead of the original estimate of $800,000, ran up to $4,212,368.50 — before it was entirely completed. The final cost was $5,000,000.
5. The walls sank at one corner fully two feet, and it was found necessary to substitute an iron cornice for the stone one contemplated in the original plan. Since then the whole building has sunk evenly about two and a half feet.
6. General Butler, when he took possession of New Orleans in 1862, established his headquarters in the Customhouse, and occupied the suite of rooms on the Decatur Street side. The upper floor of the building, though then unfinished, was used as a military prison. Mumford, the man Butler ordered hung for tearing down the United States flag from the mint, was imprisoned in a room at the foot of the staircase while awaiting trial.
7. The first U.S. Postoffice in New Orleans was established on October 1, 1803, with Blaise Cenas as postmaster. He was succeeded by Thomas B. Johnson in 1810. In August of 1810 the postoffice was moved to a building on Custom House Street between Royal and Chartres Streets. This building was formerly occupied by Tully Robinson, an attorney. In 1853 it was moved to the United States District Court on Canal Street. In 1860 it was established in the Customhouse, where it remained until the new building was erected on Camp Street opposite Lafayette Square.

The Old Louisiana Sugar and Rice Exchange stood at N. Front and Bienville Streets, New Orleans. (now demolished)

History of the Louisiana Sugar Industry

From the early part of the nineteenth century until the establishment of the Louisiana Sugar & Rice Exchange the crops of sugar, syrup and molasses of Louisiana were bought and sold at New Orleans on the levee at the foot of Bienville Street. The sugar planters shipped their products to the city on river packets, and the merchants and the brokers came prepared to buy and to argue about prices and grades. There were no laws and regulations for sampling, grading, and buying or selling sugar and its by-products. In those days sugar was sold in hogsheads of 1200 pounds, and was made by the open kettle process (it was brown sugar).

Later clarified sugar (white) was sold in barrels of 350 pounds at a fixed price per pound. Raw sugars were sold on the basis of 96 test, which means sugar 96 percent pure or with a 96 percent sucrose content. But clarified sugar was more or less discontinued, and unwashed sugar (commonly known as raw sugar) was packed 320 to 350 pounds in burlap bags. This became the standard package. Granulated sugar (or table grades), which is universally used today, is packed generally in 100-pound burlap bags, but some refineries put it up also in smaller bags of cotton or paper. The custom of packing sugar in barrels has been discontinued altogether.

In any event, trading on the levee was, to say the least, awkward, and so it became the habit of some dealers and brokers to meet under a date palm in the back yard of the residence of Isaac Delgado at 1220 Philip Street, where they could relax and talk leisurely as they sat comfortably in easy chairs and drank Scotch and soda or good bourbon whiskey. Sometimes the refreshments made them unduly optimistic, and some of them bought or sold too freely. In some cases the sale had to be cancelled, and this caused confusion, for a dealer or a broker did not know at the end of the meeting whether he had made a deal or not. In order to avoid such embarrassment, since in those days a man's word was his bond, refreshments or not, Mr. Delgado, who carried on a very extensive business in sugar, had a trading ring placed under the tree, and no man was held responsible for any trade unless he stood in the ring—but in the ring his offer was a binding contract. This same ring, having been used for many years by the Louisiana Sugar & Rice Exchange on its floor for the same purpose, is again back under the same date palm at 1220 Philip Street. This property was willed to the City of New Orleans by Isaac Delgado, and was later purchased by David W. Pipes, and is now owned by George Dinwiddie, who uses it as a residence, and preserves the trading ring as a landmark of history.

In the spring of 1883 a number of this same group who were prominent in the sugar industry of Louisiana met under this same date palm at 1220 Philip Street, and agreed to organize the Louisiana Sugar Exchange for the purpose of providing and maintaining suitable accommodations for the sale of sugar and molasses, and to establish regulatory rules; and also to devise a system of grades, to adjust controversies, and to promote the interest of the trade in general. A charter covering these and many other points was drawn up, and a building was erected at the corner of North Front and Bienville Streets, which was a short distance from the place where trading was done on the levee.

The men who met under this date palm and who signed the charter on March 6, 1883, were: E. M. Scott, Jules J. D'Aquin, R. B. Scudder, John B. Levert, Louis Bush, D. R. Calder, Sam'l. Delgado, and N. B. Trist acting as notary. Edward G. Gay was elected president.

The lot on which the building was erected was purchased from Baron Jean Dominique Bruno Armand Chaurand of Lyon, France, on July 20, 1883. The terms of the sale were unusual. The Sugar Exchange agreed to pay the Baron $850.00 a year during the remainder of his life, and upon his death the lot was to become its property. His heirs were to have no claim whatever upon it. He lived 13 years longer.

When he died the ground was, by the agreement, deeded to the Exchange, and the cost had been $12,505.00.

The building, which was dedicated on June 3, 1884, was designed by James Freret, architect, and was constructed by J. R. Turck, a contractor. The cost of the grounds and the building was well over $75,000. Bounded by Bienville, North Front, and Clay Streets, the floor covered a space 104 by 64 feet, and the center dome rose to a height of 65 feet, supported by four massive fluted Ionic columns. These columns were of solid pine, and it is not likely that any other building in New Orleans has timbers of this size. It was a remarkably fine structure, with all facilities for trading, including blackboards for reporting prices from hour to hour, a trading ring, sampling desks, offices upstairs for brokers, and a lobby that extended from one street to the other. Here the great sugar crop of Louisiana was sold every season. As sugar was the crop of Louisiana, and constituted one of the largest industries of this city, the old Louisiana Sugar Exchange was a very active institution.

But as rice became also a major crop in Louisiana, and required, as same as sugar, the establishment of rules and a place for marketing, the Louisiana Sugar Exchange offered its facilities to members of that industry, and on January 28, 1889, amended its charter and changed its name to the Louisiana Sugar & Rice Exchange. The rice industry was not, however, to play a great part in trading at this place. It was thought that a future market for rice could be established and would be of great advantage to the dealers and brokers as well as to the growers, so that they could protect their markets as the wheat farmers and dealers do. The rice brokers and dealers were very hopeful and made ready for trading. There was some buying and selling in the ordinary course, but only one future contract was made. It was not long before the traders lost interest and went back to their old methods. But the sugar industry continued to sell its crop on the floor of the Exchange, and the business transacted there was by far the largest by volume in the city. It was, in fact, the center of Louisiana's sugar industry, for here the crop was sold, policies were made, and legislative matters concerning the Louisiana sugar planters and processors were fought or supported according to the manner in which they affected the sugar interests in general.

In 1940 the Louisiana Sugar & Rice Exchange sold its building at North Front and Bienville Streets, and moved to 233 North Peters Street, occupying the entire ground floor of a building and sub-leasing spaces to the Western Union Telegraph Company and the Postal Telegraph Company (which had been its tenants in its former location). Here a fire destroyed its furniture and all its records, as well as an excellent oil painting of Etienne de Boré, which had been presented by Isaac Delgado some years before. Thus, the records being destroyed, it was impossible to procure much information which would be of interest.

But it is known that the men who served as president of the Louisiana Sugar and Rice Exchange are the following:

1833 to 1884	(first president) Edward J. Gay
1884 to 1887	Richard Milliken
1887 to 1888	Samuel Delgado
1888 to 1889	Wm. Henderson
1889 to 1891	Samuel Delgado
1891 to 1892	John B. Levert
1892 to 1894	James C. Murphy
1894 to 1895	Jas. Thibaut
1895 to 1901	James C. Murphy
1901 to 1903	John A. Wogan
1903 to 1919	*James C. Murphy
(*Elected for life but retired in 1919)	
1919 to 1932	Richard M. Murphy
1932 to 1936	Armand J. Scully
1936 to 1946	Edmund J. Garland
1946 to present time	Charles A. Levy

In 1935 a few of the older members of the Exchange sugfested that the institution be reorganized, and that its name be changed. But when the minority of the Board of Directors, many of whom were also old members, refused, those members who had made the suggestion promptly resigned. But a membership committee was formed with Charles A. Levy as chairman. Mr. Levy, being head of the Sugar Division of J. Aron & Company, had a large following in the sugar industry, and it was not long before the Louisiana Sugar & Rice Exchange had applications for many new members, more than enough to replace those who had resigned. As a matter of fact, the membership was brought up to a number greater than ever before in its history.

At the same time Lewis A. Scherck was appointed chairman of the finance committee, and with the finances of the institution in good condition under his careful direction, the building of the Exchange was repaired at a cost of several thousand dollars and old debts were paid in full. Mr. Scherck, a sugar chemist and a sugar broker as well, had been a member of the Exchange since 1890, and had always taken a very great interest in its welfare and in its progress. He had been elected 13 consecutive times as chairman of the finance committee. He also served as chairman of the chemical committee during the same time.

On November 2, 1936, Ed. J. Garland was elected president to succeed Mr. Scully. Mr. Garland was then Commissioner of Delgado-Albania, which is a sugar plantation bequeathed to the City of New Orleans by Isaac Delgado, the revenue of which was to go to the support of the Delgado Trades Schools, which this philanthropist also left to the City of New Orleans. Mr. Garland, being very active in the sugar business at the time, greatly assisted Mr. Levy, chairman of the membership committee, and through his influence a great many new members were added, and by 1937 the membership reached its peak.

By this time the character of the sugar market had changed completely. Sales were no longer made on the floor of the Exchange, for each dealer or broker traded from his office, but he used the Louisiana Sugar & Rice Exchange as a source of information, and as the official arbiter of the rules of the trade. Dealers and brokers were kept up to the minute through an official wire service to which the institution subscribed. Listed also on the blackboards were car-loadings (of sugar) which came from the railroads. The Exchange furnished the weekly and the season's average price to the planters and to the refiners. In 1935, when sugar quotas were set up under the Jones-Costigan Act, and the farmers received benefit payments based upon the average price of raw sugars, the United States Department of Agriculture used the weekly average quotations of the Louisiana Sugar & Rice Exchange to determine the price of sugarcane as a basis for making settlements.

After serving nine terms as president, Mr. Garland announced that he would not be a candidate for re-election. The nominating committee then nominated Charles A. Levy, who several years ago, upon the death of Mr. Seago, became first vice-president. Mr. Levy was elected to the presidency on November 2, 1946, and was re-elected on November 7, 1947.

In the meantime Mr. Garland became general manager of the New Orleans Public Belt Railroad, but he remained a member of the Board of Directors.

In 1948 members of the Board of Directors of the Louisiana Sugar & Rice Exchange were: Charles A. Levy, Thomas Douglas, Ed. J. Garland, Harry S. Hardin, John Keen, Irving Legendre, Stephen C. Munson, Edgar Murray, Michel Provosty, H. F. Saufley, Clarence J. Savoie, Lewis A. Scherck, Ernest A. Burguieres, and Jay Weil. The officers were: Charles A. Levy, president; Ernest A. Burguieres, first vice-president; Clarence J. Savoie, second vice-president; Lewis A. Scherck, chairman of the finance committee, and Raymond J. Martinez, secretary.

It would hardly be proper to write the historical sketch of the Louisiana Sugar & Rice Exchange without at least a passing mention of D. D. Colcock, who became its secretary at the beginning of its organization and served for nearly thirty years, during which time he became an outstanding authority on sugar and its markets, and rendered a great service to the sugar industry by its able presentation of tariff issues before the Congress of the United States. He was of great assistance in building up the Louisiana Sugar & Rice Exchange to become one of the largest organizations of its kind in America.

EARLY DISCOVERIES OF SUGAR CANE AND ITS PRODUCTS AND THE DEVELOPMENT OF THE INDUSTRY IN LOUISIANA

Sugar cane, from which molasses and sugar are made, was called the honey-making reed by the people of India. It is one of the earliest plants of which we have a record. About 4,000 years ago the Hindus cultivated it, but they did not then know how to make sugar, and were rather slow in developing a sugar-making process, for it was not until 100 A.D. that they began to export a granulated salt-like product under the name of "gravel sugar," which was used in medicine. Since the sugar contained a great quantity of molasses it possessed a great healing quality, and was considered a fine tonic. It is well known, of course, that plain sugar has healing properties.

How the people of India produced this "gravel-sugar" from cold cane juice is not known today. They most likely discovered the process accidentally, for they were philosophers, not scientists, as one would judge from their slow progress, for it was 500 years before they decided to try boiling the juice. This boiling process produced a mass of sugar grain and molasses which today is called "massecuite" in Louisiana. The boiling method of producing sugar apparently created some interest in the seventh century. Fifty years after its discovery, the process was carried into China.

It is thought that the process of refining sugar was discovered during the Middle Ages by the physicians of Arabia, in whose prescriptions sugar had an important place. It is not known what diseases they treated with sugar and molasses, but today sugar is recommended by many physicians for nausea, stomach ulcers, liver disorders, pneumonia, and to combat shock. Sometimes it is injected into the blood stream.

The Portuguese and the Spaniards were the first great cultivators of sugar cane. It was planted in Madeira as early as 1420. In the first part of the sixteenth century it was planted in the occupied territory of the West Indies and South America.

From 1500 to 1520 the sugar trade of San Domingo expanded with great rapidity. It was from the dues levied on imports of sugar and molasses brought from San Domingo to Spain that Charles V procured funds to build his palaces at Madrid and Toledo.

In the Middles Ages Venice was the great European center of the sugar trade. Toward the end of the fifteenth century a Venetian citizen received a reward of 100,000 crowns for having discovered the art of making loaf sugar.

In 1319 Tomano Loredano, a merchant of Venice, shipped 100,000 pounds of sugar to Great Britain to be exchanged for wool. That is the earliest record we have of sugar cane products on the British market.

Sugar in those days was a costly luxury, and was used only as medicine. The price (in 1319) was 1 shilling and 9½ pence (43¢) a pound. It was, of course, brown sugar, containing a good quantity of molasses, although it was called refined sugar.

A SKETCH OF THE HISTORY AND ROMANCE OF THE SUGAR AND MOLASSES INDUSTRY OF LOUISIANA

In 1751 two French ships carrying troops to Louisiana stopped at Port au Prince, St. Domingo, and the Jesuits there put on board of them some sugar cane and a few Negroes who were acquainted with the cultivation of that plant. The shipment and the Negroes reached New Orleans safely, and, in accordance with instructions, the sugar cane was planted on the plantation of the reverend fathers, which was located where now stand the great business establishments of Baronne, Carondelet, Dryades, and Rampart Streets, just above Canal Street.

Thus it can be said that the first sugar cane of Louisiana was produced by land on which the Roosevelt Hotel, the Jesuits Church, the Canal Bank Building, the Hibernia Building, and many other establishments in their vicinity, are now standing.

A fairly large crop was produced from this planting, but the experiments made to produce sugar were not successful. The plantation continued, however, to grow sugar cane for "chewing purposes," and found a ready market in the town.

For eight years the Jesuits grew sugar cane, but made no further attempts to granulate sugar from it, for they were satisfied with the money they were making. Moreover, they were religious men, not scientists.

But in 1754, Dubreuil, a wealthy planter of the colony, bought some of this sugar cane and planted it on a tract of land, a portion of which is now Esplanade Avenue. At the same time he built a sugar mill, for he believed that he could produce sugar. His venture came to nothing. For many years his sugar mill lay there rusting away as if to remind the people that Louisiana was not the place to make sugar. Still there were men who thought that if sugar could be made in the West Indies and in Central and South America it could also be made in Louisiana. One of them was the Chevalier de Mazan, who had a place on the Mississippi River not far from the city. In 1764 he made an attempt to granulate sugar, but his project, like the others, met with failure. A year later Destrehan and some other planters grew sugar cane, and, believing that they could profit by the mistakes of Dubreuil and the Chevalier de Mazan, put up a sugar mill similar to those which had been built.

They produced a substance similar to guava jelly, and while it was a wholesome food, rich in minerals and sucrose, it was not sugar. They loaded several barrels of it on a ship bound for France, but it leaked out before it reached port.

Although the colonists had not been able to produce sugar from the cane juice, they succeeded admirably in making a rum called "tafia," which seemed to please the people, for they drank great quantities of it. In an official report of June 7, 1764, d'Abbadie said that "the immoderate use of tafia has stupefied the whole population."

After the unsuccessful efforts of Destrehan and his associates, several more attempts were made to manufacture sugar in Louisiana and there were some claims of success. There were two Spaniards, Don Antonio Mendez and Solis, who planted an extensive acreage of sugar cane in St. Bernard parish. Mendez made syrup and Solis made tafia. But it is reported that Mendez bought out Solis, who came here as a refugee from St. Domingo, and then employed a sugar-maker, of Cuba, whose name was Antoine Morin. It is claimed that Mendez, with the assistance of Morin, made sugar for the first time in Louisiana, and that during many years he continued to make it.

Historians generally have taken no account of this, but in an old copy of the **Louisiana Sentinelle de Thibodeaux,** J. B. Avequin says: "In 1791 Antonio Mendez of New Orleans bought from Solis his distilling outfit, the land and the canes, with the firm resolution of devoting himself to sugar manufacture and to conquer all difficulties. For this purpose Mendez employed Antoine Morin who had passed many years in St. Domingo for the purpose of studying cane culture and sugar manufacture. But whether it was that Mendez did not have the means of establishing a sugar factory like those of St. Domingo or whether he still doubted of complete success, he made but few barrels of sugar, and it is certain that he experimented also with refining it, for in 1792 Mendez presented to Don Rendon, who was then Intendant of Louisiana for Spain, some small loaves of sugar refined by him. It required one of these loaves to sweeten two cups of coffee. At a grand dinner he gave that year to the authorities of New Orleans, Intendant Rendon called the attention of his guests to this sugar during the dessert, presenting it to them as a Louisiana product made by Antonio Mendez. Up to this time, it is thus seen, Mendez and Morin had manufactured but a very small quantity of sugar, since it was still presented as an object of curiosity."

It is well established, on testimony of other authorities in addition to the one given here, that Don Antonio Mendez, with the assistance of Antoine Morin, made the first sugar in Louisiana, and that he was also the first to refine it, but it does not seem likely that he made it in a commercial quantity.

THE ACTUAL BEGINNING OF THE LOUISIANA SUGAR INDUSTRY

The first commercial crop of sugar in Louisiana was produced by Etienne de Boré on his plantation, which is now Audubon Park, in 1794-1795. He had purchased a good quantity of sugar cane and planted it while he made all other preparations to manufacture sugar. Whether he succeeded meant a great deal to Louisiana, for the indigo crop, which had been the chief source of farm revenue, was being rapidly destroyed by an insect for which the farmers had not found a remedy, and the English, having control of India, where this product was grown in great quantities, were hard competitors. A new and profitable crop would save the colony.

But whether this cane juice would granulate by de Boré's proposed method was a question in the minds of the anxious indigo farmers. De Boré had with him Antoine Morin, who had assisted Don Antonio Mendez in making sugar, and when the time came for grinding the cane and turning the juice into sugar (if it was to be possible), a great crowd assembled at the mill. It was an excited crowd. Many were doubtful, but there were also many quite hopeful that de Boré and Morin would succeed in the venture.

As these two men stood by the boiling kettle waiting to see whether the sugar would granulate, the crowd waited with eager impatience, ready to hear the announcement of failure or success. Finally, de Boré cried out: "It granulates!" At last Louisiana was to be a sugar-producing state, and great wealth was to come to it from that industry. The first crop sold for $12,000.00, which, considering the value of money in those times, was a good sum. In 1802 New Orleans exported 4,000 hogsheads of sugar and 800 casks of molasses.

The cane from which de Boré made his first crop of sugar was sometimes called the **Malabar** or **Bengal** variety, but which became known in Louisiana as Creole cane, introduced by the Jesuits in 1751. As the production of sugar became a mighty industry in Louisiana, new varieties were introduced. In 1856 the Congress made a special appropriation for the purpose of procuring cuttings of sugar cane of such varieties best suited to the soil and climate of Louisiana.

This appropriation was made after a poor yield over a period of several years, and it was generally believed that the varieties of sugar cane cultivated in Louisiana had "run out." Many varieties were imported from the West Indies and South America. Later (1872) sugar cane for seeding purposes was imported from Java and also from Japan. But these "foreign varieties," as they were called by the planters of Louisiana, did not improve the yield to any great extent. The yield was only improved when it was discovered that cane here would germinate and produce seedlings. It was a process of selection; that is, selecting from the seedlings, the cane which promised a larger yield and a greater sugar content. A sugar experiment station was established at Audubon Park, and here many new varieties of cane were produced, which proved to be of great benefit to the sugar industry of Louisiana. Many years ago this station was moved to the Louisiana State University at Baton Rouge, where the finest sugar school in the world is located, and here students from all parts of the globe come to study sugar culture and manufacturing.

The Sugar Mill

The first steam-propelled mill in Louisiana was built in 1822 by John J. Coiron. Previously the mills had been operated by horsepower. In that day steam engines of a size sufficient to grind cane had to be imported at a cost of $12,000 each. Only the wealthy sugar planters could use them. But soon the foundries of this country began to produce steam engines. The cost was brought down to $5,000, and by 1828 there were 82 mills using steam power.

Improvements were rapidly made in the sugar mills, and from a rather crude beginning they became factories scientifically operated. The vacuum pan process of making sugar and molasses was introduced in 1830, and was immediately successful.

Other improved machinery and better methods of processing sugar were later developed and those of the old-time sugar mills which were not remodeled with new sugar-making equipment slowly ceased to operate. In 1853 there were 1,481 sugar mills operating in Louisiana, the greatest number that ever existed, and they produced 224,118 tons of sugar. But in

1894 only 449 mills produced 317,306 tons. Today 57 mills, all large and modern, produce a yearly average of 550,000 tons of sugar and 30 million gallons of molasses of a better grade than was ever produced in Louisiana or in any other country.

The invention of the vacuum pan by E. C. Howard of England about 1813 was a step forward in the processing of sugar. But more important was Norbert Rillieux's invention (in 1845) of the multiple-effect evaporation for concentrating cane juice. It was a great labor-saving affair, which lowered the cost, and lightened sugar's color. Norbert Rillieux was born on March 17, 1806, the son of a wealthy engineer and planter. His mother was a slave on his father's plantation. Noticing that he possessed superior intelligence, his father sent him to be educated in France, where he became an instructor, and published several scientific papers. He returned to New Orleans, and worked out a new technique for handling sewage. This would have been a boon to yellow fever-ridden New Orleans had the process been adopted, but it was not. He died in Paris on October 8, 1894.

Life on the Sugar Plantations of Louisiana

On every sugar plantation stands a mansion similar to those of England or France during the days of the feudal system. Since the centralization of the industry there are many old castles in the sugar belt, abandoned and in ruins, but still in the fading picture of the old-time plantation life.

The modern sugar mill, with its extreme methods of sanitation and efficient machinery, has lost the romantic aspect of earlier days. Once the social life of the sugar belt was in full swing during the grinding season, and the old mansions were filled with visitors for whom sugar-house parties were arranged. The entertainment on a sugar-house party consisted of serving hot cane juice, sometimes spiked with rum, or eating sugar cane and walking through the sugar mill to watch the process of making molasses and sugar.

In those days (the middle of the nineteenth century) the sugar industry of Louisiana had grown to so great an enterprise that it stimulated trade not only in New Orleans, but also throughout the entire Mississippi Valley. The greatest portion of products shipped to New Orleans was not for export, but was sent to the plantations of Louisiana where thousands of slaves had to be clothed and fed, and where a lavish style of living was maintained. The great demands of the plantations actually taxed the resources of New Orleans, and the banks found it difficult to supply the cash required in the operation of so many large enterprises to whom no one dared refuse credit.

In his book, *The Creoles of Louisiana*, George W. Cable gives his reader the impression that all the sugar planters of Louisiana were Creoles, but this is not correct, for while the majority of them were of French and Spanish descent, there were many of Anglo-Saxon stock who came from New England, Kentucky, Tennessee, and Virginia.

LOUISIANA SUGAR AND MOLASSES MILL — 1853

The description which he gave of the Louisiana Creole applied also to the Anglo-Saxon planter of Louisiana. He said: "The brow and cheek of this man were darkened by outdoor exposure, but they were not weather-beaten. His shapely, bronzed hand was no harder or rougher than was due to the use of the bridle-rein and the gunstock . . . His speech was positive, his manner was military, his sentiment was antique, his clothing was of broadcloth, his boots were neat, and his hat was soft, broad and slouched a little to show its fineness. Such in his best aspect was the Mississippi River planter. When sugar was his crop, and Creole-French his native tongue, his polish would sometimes be finer still, with a finish got in Paris."

In the days of which Cable writes the life of the sugar planter was easy. He was a man of leisure, who frequently completed his education at the University of Virginia or Harvard, if not in Paris. Sometimes he became a lawyer or physician, but with no definite intention of practicing his profession, for he did not have to earn a living by means of it.

During the summer when the cane was ripening in the fields, the sugar planter went away on vacation. In this period, when the crops were laid by, the Negroes, mostly idle, spent their time amusing themselves in their own way, usually in fishing and hunting. Or they loafed at the plantation stores, and bought whatever the store-keeper would sell them on credit. Their wants were great, but their needs were small, for their houses were furnished them free of cost, and they had the use of land to make a garden. In addition fuel was free to them if they got it out of the forests. Living was not a problem, but a "nick'l box o' sa'dines, a loaf o' bread, and a pack o' 'bacco" on credit satisfied them immensely.

Before summer was ended the plantation owners returned home from their vacations, and the Negroes, by this time low in pocket change, and deep in debt, were called back to work. Great preparations had to be made for the approaching grinding season. Large quantities of wood had to be hauled from the forest for fuel in the sugar mill and for homes on the plantation. The harness had to be mended, the mules shod, and all vehicles had to be put in order. The workmen in the sugar mills were busy during this time repairing machinery, and testing every instrument which contributed toward the making of sugar, for when the mill once began operation it continued to run twenty-four hours a day, and stopped only on Sunday.

The great boarding houses for the outside workers who came "to make grinding," were made ready for business. Several old mammies got busy shining up the pots and generally putting things in readiness, making sure that the coffee pots above all were put in good order, for this mild stimulant was very much in demand. The workers in the mill came many times a day to partake of the old mammy's coffee. And this made her proud. Her meals also brought praise, for she knew how to cook — or she was not an old mammy of the plantation.

But those old days have gone, and the manner of living on the Louisiana sugar plantations today is different. The paved highways, and the swift automobiles have brought the plantation dwellers closer to the city, and the moving picture shows have made a change in the home-life.

The sugar mills are scientifically operated with highly skilled workers, and have chemists to test every substance that contributes to the manufacture of molasses and sugar.

MOLASSES AND SUGAR BRING WEALTH
IN LOUISIANA

Within ten years after Etienne de Boré produced the first "commercial" crop of sugar, the planters of Louisiana began to amass fortunes. Governor Wm. C. C. Claiborne wrote to Thomas Jefferson that "the facility with which the sugar planters amass wealth is almost incredible." It seems that many found it more profitable to produce rum, which was also a great source of revenue, for in 1802 the surrounding parishes supplied the New Orleans market with 14,000,000 gallons of that "alcoholic beverage."

In 1816 the *Niles Weekly Register* reported that "sugar and molasses and rum will soon be to the United States what cotton now is. Louisiana will shortly supply more than our domestic wants require." Land suitable for sugar cane was at that time valued at from $300 to $500 an acre.

Ten years later (1826) there were 82 steam operated sugar factories and 408 operated by horsepower. In 1850 there were 865 steam and 681 horsepower sugar mills operating, and in that year 134,884 tons of raw sugar and 12,000,000 gallons of molasses were produced. The sugar sold at 3½ cents a pound, and molasses at 20 cents a gallon, which at today's money value would be more than 40 cents a gallon.

The production of molasses increased rapidly up to the time of the War Between the States. In 1860 the production was 17,858,100 gallons; in 1861 it was 18,414,550 gallons; in 1862 it was 36,982,505 gallons.

For the season of 1861-62 there were 1,027 steam sugar mills and 264 horsepower sugar mills operating in Louisiana, and they produced 459,410 hogsheads of sugar. The average weight of a hogshead was 1,150 pounds.

The War Between the States paralyzed the sugar industry of Louisiana, as it did all other industries, and during the last year of the struggle (1865) the production of sugar was only 10,662 hogsheads and production of molasses was 16,000 gallons, less than 10 percent of the normal production.

But the sugar industry was the first to come back in Louisiana. New varieties of cane were introduced, and improved equipment for sugar mills was provided. New systems were devised for clarifying the juice, and for making molasses and sugar.

LEADING MEN IN THE HISTORY OF THE LOUISIANA SUGAR INDUSTRY

To Etienne de Boré goes the credit for producing the first commercial crop of sugar and molasses. The sugar planters who followed him are responsible for developing the industry. Many of them turned their attention to finding new and better varieties of cane; and they also agitated for appropriations from the government to carry on experimental work in this connection.

John J. Coiron organized the **Agricultural Society of Georgia,** and succeeded in persuading the legislature of that state to assist in research and experimental work in the selection of new canes. In 1817 he himself brought in the Striped and Purple varieties, which were found to be superior to the Creole varieties grown exclusively at that time in Louisiana.

In 1872 P. M. LaPice went to Java and brought back cane which is often called by his name, but which in Java is known as **Canne Penache.** He was the first to put in a double pressure mill to extract nearly all the juice from the cane, making the bagasse immediately ready for use. It was then used as a fertilizer. Later it was in some cases used for fuel. Now it is used for many purposes. Celotex and insulating board are made from it, and many nurseries use bagasse as a substitute for peat moss, and find it very satisfactory.

Among other prominent planters during the Golden Age of Sugar and Molasses was Valcour Aime, who was the first to install vacuum pans, and who kept a diary of his day by day activities in the cultivation of sugar cane and the production of sugar which today is very interesting reading. He was also the first to use coal in his sugar mill.

In more recent years such men as Pipes, Krumbhaar, and Hones donated to their fellow-sugar planters 25 percent of a very valuable supply of seed-cane of excellent variety, at a time when the Louisiana planters were greatly discouraged because of the small yield and the advance of the cane-borer.

Among other noteworthy men in the history of the sugar industry of Louisiana was Leon Godchaux, a native of Herbeville, France, who arrived at New Orleans in 1824, and who was to play an important part in the development of the sugar and molasses industry of the state. First he became a leading merchant, noted for his generosity, his interest in public affairs, and for his genius in industry.

In 1862 he bought his first plantation, then known as the Antoine Boudousquie Plantation, and which is now the location of the Reserve Refinery and the Reserve factory. (owned by Godchaux-Henderson Sugar Co. Inc.)

The sugar planters of the middle nineteenth century were very hospitable, for they took pride in their breeding and good manners. And hospitality is kindness, as Mr. Leon Godchaux correctly considered, for it happened that while he was a traveling merchant he fell ill on the Boudousquie Plantation, and was given the most considerate care, for he knew how to accept favors graciously. Some years later, when Mr. Boudousquie could no longer afford to own the plantation, Mr. Godchaux bought it, but because of the kindness he had received, he permitted the Boudousquie family to remain on the place as long as any member survived. The family lived there for many years after Mr. Godchaux bought the place, free of rent or any other obligation.

Leon Godchaux built the first central sugar mill in Louisiana to grind the cane of the small sugar cane growers of the surrounding territory who could sell to a central factory more profitably than they could grind themselves to make sugar and molasses in a small open-kettle mill.

This was, of course, the beginning of the great enterprise of Godchaux Sugars, Inc., which has carried out the traditional policies of its founder since his death in 1899.

From the early part of the 19th century to about 1865 P. A. Champomier issued in the form of a booklet an annual "Statement of the Sugar Crop Made in Louisiana." He identified the locations of the plantations by naming them and giving the distance by river from New Orleans, and he set forth opposite each one the number of 1,000-pound hogsheads produced. In 1845 the largest sugar planters of the state were T. W. Chinn of West Baton Rouge, Lucien Marionneaux of Myrtle Grove Plantation and Michael Schlatre of Hunter's Lodge Plantation in Iberville parish, and D. F. Kenner and D. S. Bringier of Ascension.

Most of the planters produced from 40 to 500 hogsheads around the middle of the century. But in 1859 the crops were somewhat larger. In that year Edward J. Gay of St. Louis Plantation in Iberville parish produced 1,275 hogsheads, which was one of the largest crops in the state.

What happened to these plantations a hundred years later would make an interesting story, but this is not the place for it. A few are still owned and operated by the descendants of the former owners, but most of them have fallen into the hands of others, or have become part of a large syndicate.

OTHER NOTABLE MEN OF THE LOUISIANA SUGAR INDUSTRY

Some other men of eminence in the sugar industry's glorious period were: Charles A. Farwell, Richard Milliken, Gen. William Porcher Miles, Judge P. A. Rost, Lucien Marionneaux and Brothers. (The Marionneaux family of Iberville Parish owned around 3,000 acres of land, and were for four generations among the largest manufacturers of sugar in Louisiana. Lucien Marionneaux owned Myrtle Grove plantation at Plaquemine, which he sold in 1880, and purchased Olivia plantation in West Baton Rouge Parish. This family first settled in the West Florida parishes around 1750, and some members later moved to Iberville, where they received large Spanish grants.) J. W. Beasley owned Wildwood plantation at Napoleonville. Also among the large producers of sugar were W. E. Howell of Thibodaux; August Levert of West Baton Rouge Parish; Harry L. Laws of West Baton Rouge Parish, owner of Cinclare plantation; John Hill of Port Allen, was one of the most prominent sugar planters of West Baton Rouge Parish.

The Bartons were among the most prominent sugar planters of the Lafourche section. Elijah D. Barton came to Louisiana from Tennessee around the middle of the nineteenth century as a mere boy, and found work on a sugar plantation at Napoleonville. The owner, seeing that he was manifestly a well bred lad, took him in the house to live with his family, and he applied himself so diligently to the study of the cultivation of sugar cane and the manufacture of sugar, he soon became manager of the plantation. He later bought St. Clair plantation in St. James Parish, which he operated successfully until his death. His sons all became owners of large sugar plantations, and were known throughout the community as men of sterling qualities. Ernest H. Barton owned St. Emma plantation (of 13,000 acres and a sugar mill) on Bayou Lafourche, a few miles from Donaldsonville. His residence, a beautiful colonial dwelling, is still standing, and faces the road along the bayou, which being so thickly populated for many miles is called the "longest street in the world." Clarence Barton owned Little Texas plantation, which is one of the largest in the area of Napoleonville. He owned at one time several other plantations in addition to Little Texas. Walter Barton owned Riverside, of 1,000 acres and sugar mill in Ascension Parish, near Donaldsonville. And Elijah D. Barton's daughter, Mrs. E. L. Pike, operated St. Clair plantation after his death for many years. Carroll Barton owned Magnolia plantation on Bayou Lafourche. The Beasley family owned Wildwood plantation on Bayou Lafourche. (Both Clarence Barton and Ernest H. Barton married Beasley girls of this family.)

"Little Texas" plantation in Assumption Parish, which was owned and operated by Clarence C. Barton, lies within the old historic "League Square," — a tract of land granted to a Catholic priest by the Spanish government for religious purposes. Titles of land within this square can be traced to the time of the Spanish grant, hence the question of their validity has never arisen. On this plantation is a large Indian mound, which was used as a burial ground by the Pugh and Phillips families. Its center was marked by a large live oak, entirely sheltering, with its massive outstretched limbs, the graves beneath.

EXCERPTS FROM CHAMPOMIER'S SUGAR GUIDE

From around 1846 to 1862 P. A. Champomier issued a booklet annually, which was entitled STATEMENT OF THE SUGAR CROP MADE IN LOUISIANA. He identified the plantations by giving the names of the parishes in which they were located, and the distance they were from New Orleans (in miles along the river). The River Parishes were arranged so as to commence first on the right side (the right side is west of the river, and the left side is on the east). Each book contains about 50 pages, with a preface which describes the condition of the crop. This preface was written in English and French, for apparently there were many people of that period in the sugar industry who did not understand English.

It is noteworthy that Louisiana's production of sugar during the first year of the Civil War was greater than it had ever been before. With 1,291 sugar mills operating in 1858 the outturn was 362,296 hogsheads*, as compared to 459,410 in 1861. It is true, that the sugar cane had already been processed when New Orleans surrendered to Farragut on April 25, 1862 but it is remarkable that the industry, with so many men of the sugar belt away at war, could produce so great an amount of sugar.

* — (A hogshead weighs from 1,000 to over 1,150 lbs. These figures are based on 1,150 lbs. hogsheads, which Champomier considered a fair estimate, for some hogsheads weighed more than 1,150 lbs., and some slightly less than 1,000 lbs.)

The few pages of these books reproduced here are of the parishes with the largest outturn of sugar for the years 1846 and 1862. These pages show the names of many early sugar planters whose descendants are probably living in Louisiana.

A TYPICAL PLANTATION HOME.

EAST BATON-ROUGE—CONTINUED.

LEFT SIDE.

NAMES OF PLANTERS AND PARISHES.	Distance from City.	No. of Hhds.	No. of 1000 lbs. nett
Genl. Jos. Bernard	141	—	—
Perkins, Bros	130	472	655
M. L. Meaker 1847-8	"	—	—
Mrs Combe	"	90	105
Amos, Adams & Co. 1846-7	"	—	—
Revd. M. Vancourt 1847-8	"	—	—
Bernard Bayley	"	—	—
J. B. Scudder 1846-7	"	—	—
Rickett & Harris	"	—	—
Denis Dègre & Mother 1847-8	"	—	—
Andrew Klempetre 1846-7	"	—	—
Michel Bouillon	"	12	14
J. B. Klempetre	"	202	240
J. & H. Thomas 2d.	"	—	—
Robert Penny, 1846-7	"	—	—
Jonni Klempetre,	"	59	64
F. & G. Klempetre, 1847-8	"	—	—
Jacob Smith, 1846-7	"	—	—
Philip Garrigg,	"	—	—
Chambers & Fisk,	127	200	200
Stephen Henderson,	126	326	390
Dr. J. C. Williams,	125	188	210
Col. Philip Hickey,	124	140	160
Caldwell & Hickey	123	139	145
F. D. Conrad & A. L. Duncan	121	434	470
Joseph Bernard,	120	136	146
Estate of P. Martinez	"	59	68
Abraham Bird,	119	414	414
Julien Landry & Victor Hude,	118	11	13
Soeliène Allain,	117	376	450
Gilbert Dègre,	"	48	48
Mrs. Laurent Dègre & Son 1846-7	116	—	—
Mrs. F. Duplantier,	"	395	450
Josiah Barker,	115	304	380
Genl. Davenport & Cavelier,	"	210	220
W. B. Walker, 1847-8	"	—	—
Total Left side,		**4,222**	**4,856**

IBERVILLE.—RIGHT SIDE.

NAMES OF PLANTERS AND PARISHES.	Distance from City.	No. of Hhds.	No. of 1000 lbs. nett
Moses Brown,	116	10	11
L. L. & C. L. & V. Landry	"		

IBERVILLE.—RIGHT SIDE CONTINUED.

NAMES OF PLANTERS AND PARISHES.	Distance from City.	No. of Hhds.	No. of 1000 lbs. nett
Rd Rimes,	115	102	110
V. Comeau & F. Hébert,	"	33	36
R. Dupuy,	114	118	160
Mrs. Hébert & son,	113	144	160
L. Desobry,	"	244	270
F. Marionneau, 1846-7	"	3	3
P. Dupuy,	"	164	185
L. Marionneau 1847-8	"	—	—
J. Schelatre,	112	336	370
M. Schelatre, Sr.	"	287	355
Mrs. Wm. Dodd & son, Bayou Jacquot,	"	123	145
Mrs. L. Robertson,	"	222	255
Jas. H. Robertson,	"	140	150
Chs. Klempetre, 1847-8	"	—	—
M. Schelatre Jr. "	"	—	—
Jos. Klempetre & Brook, Bayou Plaquemines,	111	102	120
Alexander Roth,	"	34	38
Dupuy & Mill, do	"	255	285
J. A. Dardenne, do	"	233	280
Dupuy, Nerault & Co. do	"	78	90
Bissell & Schelatre, do 1847-8	"	—	—
Mathern Braud & Clemandeau, B. Gr. Tête.	124	140	160
Miles Bri-tow, 1846-7	"	—	—
David Holliday, 1817-8	"	—	—
A. Hotard & Labuve do 1846-7	"	—	—
F. Pelicher & R. Bougère do	"	—	—
Greaud & Dègre do	"	245	275
Mrs. & C. A. Slake, do	"	241	280
D. R. Orillon, do 1847-8	"	—	—
Dr. G. W. Campbell do 1846-7	"	—	—
C. P. Dickinson, do 1847-8	"	—	—
Isaac Irwin, do 1846-7	"	—	—
Austin Woolfolk, do	"	—	—
Batey & Downing do 1847-8	"	—	—
Edward & Whitall do	110	264	290
Mesmer Rills & N. Marionneau,	"	22	22
Rills & Bruslé,	"	255	300
Col. Hynes & Craighead,	109	626	710
Col. Hynes & Graighead,	"	360	415
Dr. Stone,	"	356	410
Paul Dupuy & son,	"	349	400
Mrs. R. John,	108	171	195
Ely LeBlanc,	"	46	52
A. Trier & Sherburne	"		

NAMES OF PLANTERS AND PARISHES.		Distance from City.	No. of Hhds.	No. of 1000 lbs. nett.
IBERVILLE.—RIGHT SIDE CONTINUED.				
Clarke Adams,		108	32	36
Dr. J. Clement & Casimir Berret,		107	115	126
Valery Hébert,		106	246	260
H. Degrs,		105	105	130
Jas. Porter.		104	13	12
V. & Amand Hébert,		102	175	165
Major E. G. W. Butler,		101	264	280
Landry Bros & Co.		"	198	200
Mrs. J. M. Lambremont & Z. Braud.		100	95	108
Ulger Beaugnon,	1846–7	"		
J. Allain & V. Gallaghar,		99	112	120
J. B. Braud & Bros.		"	42	48
Jos. Henry,		"	27	30
Paul Hébert & sons,		"	355	380
D. M. Wilson, Bayou Goula,		"	116	132
Rosemond Lambremont, do		"	74	83
W. C. S. Vantress, do	1847–8	"		
John D. Hamilton, do		"	60	66
Sewell & Hudson, do		"	174	210
John Garlick, do		"	144	160
Randolph & Thorton, do		"	294	335
Alvares Fisk,		"	306	360
Julien Comeau,		"	7	7
Mrs. & Joachim Comeau & Hébert,		"	102	118
Dr. Doyle,		"	130	145
Jos. A. Hébert,		98	66	75
F. D. Landry,	1846–7	"		
S. C. Pollard & Co.,		97	264	290
John Navy,		"	66	72
Abraham Billings,	1846–7	98		
Mrs. Vaughan & Hebert,		97	105	115
George Deslhonde,		"	442	475
Sigur, Brothers, (back)	1847–8	"		
Norbert Cropper,		96	72	80
Samuel T. Harrison, (back)		"	290	315
Mrs. Cyprien Ricard & Son,		95	194	215
C. Adams,		"	292	310
Mrs. Cropper and Son, (back)		"	192	215
John Andrews,		"	450	500
Mrs. E. Laure.		94	315	300
A. Sigur,		93	385	420
Thompson & Montgomery's,		92	495	530
Total right side			12,800	14,279

NAMES OF PLANTERS AND PARISHES.		Distance from City.	No. of Hhds.	No. of 1000 lbs. nett.
IBERVILLE.—LEFT SIDE.				
T. N. Brown,		114	228	300
Chas. Devenport & C. Maxent,		"	22	28
A. Christain,	1846–7	112		
Dupuy & Barker,		"	100	115
Mrs. J. & Thos. Brown,		108	64	64
John Terrell & Dr. Romer,		"		
Gourier & Anger,		105	178	220
Trasimond Aucoin & Mrs. LeBlanc,		"		
Andre LeBlanc,		"	64	72
R. McGavock,		"	47	52
R. A. Stewart,		"	100	115
Wm. H. Avery,		104	290	290
A. Delaune & Mrs. E. LeBlanc,		"	10	10
Timoleon Boissar,		"	14	14
Edward Moore,		"	180	180
A. Dupuy,		"	130	145
Simon LeBlanc,		"	84	80
Gedeon Dupuy,		"	42	40
Dr. Js. Pritchard,		103	143	165
S. LeBlanc & Artaud,		"	63	70
Mrs. L. Lessassier & Co.,		"	40	44
Ursin Joly,		101	65	70
J. Walsh and Mrs. F. Landry,	1846–7	100		
Allain & Babin,		"		
R. Arnous,		99	74	80
S. Woodward,		"	196	215
R. P. Gaillard,		98	48	52
John Hagan, Jr.,		"	62	72
R. C. Camp,		96	220	240
J. Blanchard & A. Landry,	1846–7	94	260	305
J. Blanchard,	1847–8	92		
Dr. Winfree & Upton,	1847–8	91		
Z. & D. Blouen & Co.,	1846–7	"		
Mrs. Gorham & Poché,		"	63	63
John Gardner, New River,		"	20	20
Ursin Hebert, "		"	18	18
Left side			2,824	3,138
Right side			12,800	14,279
Total Parish Iberville,			15,624	17,417

8

PARISH OF EAST BATON ROUGE.

LEFT SIDE OF MISSISSIPPI RIVER—CONTINUED.

Post Office	Names of Planters and Parishes	Distance from New Orleans	Number of Hogsheads
14–30	Thompson J. Bird, *s*, ...COMITE		120
	James Bogan, *s*, ...RIVER		49
	Major S. Robert, *s*, ...ROADS.		
	Pierre Poutz, *s*, ...[St. Tammany Parish.]		52
	Total Amount—Parish of East Baton Rouge.		4906

PARISH OF IBERVILLE.

RIGHT SIDE OF MISSISSIPPI RIVER.

Post Office	Names of Planters and Parishes	Distance from New Orleans	Number of Hogsheads
Rosedale Post Office	P. R. Ventress, *s*, ...BAYOU	R	90
	Mrs. P. B. Key and Son, *s*, ...		35
	Durald & Bogan, *s*, ...		180
	E. Woolfolk, West Oak, *s*, ...MARINGOUIN.	L	125
	Capt. Jessee Hart, Sunny Side Plant, *s*, BAYOU GROSSE TETE.	R	206
	Mrs. Emily Woolfolk, Mound Plant., *s*,	"	385
	Isaac Erwin, *s*, ...	"	205
	Mrs. A. M. Dickinson, Live Oak Plant.*s*	"	134
	Dr. G. W. Campbell, *s*, ...	"	270
	T. Johnston & Co., *s*, ...	R & L	221
	Hotard & Labauve, *s*, ...	R	125
16	C. A. Slack, Bay Farm Plantation, *s*, ...	R	205
	Keep & Schlatre, Bear Den Plant, *s*, ...	L	150
	Hotard & Labauve, *s*, ...	"	275
	Lévéque & Bujole, China Grove Pl., *s*, BAYOU	"	72
	Adolphe Dupuy & Orillon, *s*, ...	R	47
	Daniel Holliday, *s*, ...GROSSE	L	59
	Charles Booksh, *s*, ...	"	56
	Charles Kleinpeter, *s*, ...TETE.	"	55
	Roane & Hart, *s*, ...[Grand River.]		17
	Justinien Michel, *s*, ...		
	Joseph Bollinger, *h*, ...		20
	G. Micheltree & Co., *s*, ...PIGEON.		77
	Nettleton & Laughlin, *s*, ...		95
	Bissel & Schlatre, *s*, ...BAYOU	"	112
	Mrs. Paulin Dupuy, Milly Pl. *s*, PLAQUEMINE.	"	280
			270

9

PARISH OF IBERVILLE.

RIGHT SIDE OF MISSISSIPPI RIVER—CONTINUED.

Post Office	Names of Planters and Parishes	Distance from New Orleans	Number of Hogsheads
Plaquemine Post Office	Aléxandre Roth, *s*, ...BAYOU	L	114
	Joseph Kleinpeter, *s*, ...PLAQUEMINE	"	29
	M. Schlatre, Jr., Enterprise Pl., *s*	111	150
	Mrs. E. Robertson, Hunter's Lodge ......BAYOU		
	Plantation, *s*, ...JACQUOT.	"	165
	John Schlatre, *s*, ...	"	380
	Lucien Marionneaux & Co., Myrtle		
	Grove Plantation, *s*, ...	"	370
	A. Gréaud, *s*, ...	"	180
	C. L. Landry and others, *s*, ...	116	87
	E. D. Woods, Reamsland Plantation, *s*, ...	115	150
	Baltazar Dupuy, *s*, ...	114	170
	Michel Hébert & Co., *s*, ...	113	310
	Louis Désobry, *s*, ...	"	280
	F. Marionneaux, Southern Rights Pl., *s*, ...	112	200
	V. J. Dupuy, *s*, ...	"	150
	A. P. Marionneaux, *s*, ...	112	280
	Mrs. C. Schlatre, *s*, ...	111	300
	Gervais & Romain Schlatre, Homestead Pl., *s*	"	420
	Désobry Bros., *s*, ...	110	205
	Estate of W. E. Edwards, Pecan Plant., *s*	"	110
	R. C. Downes, True Hope Plantation, *s*, ...	"	115
	Edward J. Gay, St. Louis Plantation, *s*, ...	109	664
	Craighead & Johnston, *s*, ...	108	411
	Dr. J. P. R. Stone, Evergreen Plantation, *s*	107	285
	Mrs. Thos. R. Lawes, *s*, ...	"	150
	Judge J. L. Cole, Rebecca Plantation, *s*, ...	106	305
	L. Landry & Toffier, *s*, ...	"	60
	Moore & Bissell, *s*, ...	"	105
	Adams & Austin, *s*, ...	"	72
	Dr. C. Clement, *s*, ...	"	47
	Louis Hébert & Co., Plaisance Plant, *s*, ...	105	120
	E. T. Cropper Arcadia Plantation, *s*, ...	"	73
	Petit & Allain, *s*, ...	104	57
14	Auguste Lever, *s*, ...	103	225
	Whaly & Hall, Palo Alto Plantation, *s*, ...	101	182
	Col. E. G. W. Butler, Dunboyne Plant., st. pan	100	220
	B. A. Landry & Co., *s*, ...	"	174
	Mrs. P. M. Lambremont, *s*, ...	"	73
	E. Comeaux, *s*, ...	"	159
	J. B. Braud, ...	99	63

11

NAMES OF PLANTERS AND PARISHES.	Distance from New Orleans.	Number of Hogsheads.
PARISH OF IBERVILLE		
LEFT SIDE OF MISSISSIPPI RIVER—CONTINUED.		
André Leblanc, *s*	105	68
James Pritchard, *s*	104	50
A. & J. Vivez, *h* .... [Bayou Paul.]	"	28
Wm. H. Avery, *s*	"	170
Henry Vonphul, Jr., Willow Glen Plant., *s*	103	95
Edward Moore, *s*	"	185
Chas. A. Bruslé, Monticello Plantation, *s*	102	75
Jules Leblanc, Home Place, *s*	"	108
Madame Gédéon Dupuy, *s*	101	85
Mrs. Geo. Mather & Sons, Evergreen plat, *s*	"	100
Célestin Leblanc, Star Plantation, *s*	"	140
Dr. Dupuy, *h*	100	70
Mrs. Ursin Joly, *h*.. *	"	40
Mrs. Victor Babin, *h*	99	40
R. Arnous, Virginia Plantation, *s*	"	100
Joe Walsh, *h*	98	215
Estate John Hagan, Jr, *s*	96	283
R. C. Camp, open steam train.	94	61
Ursin Babin & Co., *s*	93	
Joe Walsh, *h*	"	15
Joachim Blanchard, *h*	92	78
W. T. Boote, *h*	"	00
J. T. Cambre, *h*	"	205
Mrs. R. A. Upton & Co., Rescue Plant, *s*	92	66
Clement Chastant, Revenue Plantation, *s*	"	12
Alexis Poché & Zénon Blonen, *t*	91	
Total—Parish of Iberville—Left side....		3477
PARISH OF ASCENSION		
RIGHT SIDE OF MISSISSIPPI RIVER.		
J. R. Thompson & Co., Chatham Plant., *s*	90	185
N. Mélançon, *s*	89	92
Emile Babin & Bros., *s*	"	65
Dr. Edward Duffel, Mulberry Grove Plant., *s*	88	191
W. C. S. Venitess, *s*	87	190
H. L. Duffel, *s*	86	118
Bujole & Co., *s*	"	33
Adelard Landry, Agent, *s*	85	75
J. N. Dugas.		33

Post Office: Iberville Post Office, New River P. O.—14

10

NAMES OF PLANTERS AND PARISHES.	Distance from New Orleans.	Number of Hogsheads.
PARISH OF IBERVILLE		
RIGHT SIDE OF MISSISSIPPI RIVER—CONTINUED.		
Joseph Henry, *s*	99	28
Governor P. O. Hébert, *s*	"	290
Downes & Hamilton, *s* .....BAYOU GOULA.	98	15
Hudson & Randolph, Blythewood Pl, *s*	"	150
W. C. S. Ventress, Augusta Plantation, *s*	"	750
John H. Randolph, Forest Home Plantation, steam battery	"	500
Nathaniel Cropper & Co., Tally-ho Plant., *s*	"	290
Dr. H. G. Doyle, Eureka Plantation, *s*	"	157
J. A. & T. Sigur, *s*	97	60
J. H. Randolph, Nottoway Plantation, *s*	"	160
Dubuclet & Durand, *s*	"	290
H. Rantiford, *s*	97	60
W. M. Thompson, Thérésa Plant., *s* { BACK. }	"	183
J. A. & T. Sigur Richland Pl, *s* { OFF THE }	"	435
Amadeo Roth, *s* .... { RIVER. }	"	35
George Dealhonde, *s*	"	53
Mrs. H. L. Vaughan, White Castle Plant., *s*	96	545
Dr. J. P. R. Stone, Residence Plant., *s*	"	312
Mrs. C. Ricard & Sons, *s* {open	95	235
P. C. Ricard & Mother, Annandale Pl., {steam	"	512
Mrs. Julia Cropper, Laurel Ridge Plant. *s* {train.	"	105
Mrs. C. Adams, *s*	94	287
John Andrews, vespanidus battery	93	530
Mrs. E. Lauve, Celeste Plantation, *s*	"	385
J. A. & T Sigur, Old Hickory Plantation, *s*	92	220
J. R. Thompson & Co., Claiborne Plant., *s*	91	160
Total Amount Parish of Iberville—Right side		18123
PARISH OF IBERVILLE		
LEFT SIDE OF MISSISSIPPI RIVER.		
Estate James N. Brown, *s*	113	600
F. J. Papineau, *s*	112	18
F. B. Conrad & Towles, *s*	111	54
M. & F. Martinez, *s*	108	52
Dr. Gourier & Anger, *s*	106	440
Randall McGavock, *s*	105	24

Post Office: Bayou Goula Post Office

PUBLISHED SOURCES

Dart, Henry P. (ed.). "Almonester's Will, Spanish Judicial Records of Louisiana, 1794." *Louisiana Historical Quarterly*, VI, No. 1 (January, 1923), 21-34.

——————————, and Laura L. Porteous (trans.). "The Spanish Procedure in Louisiana in 1800 for Licensing Doctors and Surgeons." *Louisiana Historical Quarterly*, XVII (1934), 294-305.

Faye, Stanley (ed.). "Louis DeClouet's Memorial to the Spanish Government, December 7, 1814." *Louisiana Historical Quarterly*, XXII, No. 3 (July, 1939), 795-818.

Holmes, Jack D. L. (ed.). *Documentos inéditos para la historia de la Luisiana, 1792-1810* (Madrid, 1963).

——————————. "The New Orleans Yellow Fever Epidemic of 1796 as Seen by the Baron de Pontalba." *The Alabama Journal of Medical Sciences*, II, No. 2 (April, 1965), 205-15.

Nasatir, Abraham P. (ed.). "Royal Hospitals in Colonial Spanish America." *Annals of Medical History*, Third Series, IV, No. 6 (1942), 481-503.

Porteous, Laura L. (trans.). "Sanitary Conditions in New Orleans Under the Spanish Régime, 1799-1800." *Louisiana Historical Quarterly*, XV, No. 4 (October, 1932), 610-17.

Robertson, James Alexander (ed.). *Louisiana Under the Rule of Spain, France, and the United States, 1785-1807.* 2 vols. Cleveland, 1911.

Rowland, Dunbar (ed.) and A. G. Sanders (trans.). *Mississippi Provincial Archives*, French Dominion. 3 vols. Jackson, Miss., 1927-1932.

Stoddard, Major Amos. *Sketches, Historical and Descriptive of Louisiana*, Philadelphia, 1812.

SECONDARY SOURCES. BOOKS

Burson, Caroline Maude. *The Stewardship of Don Esteban Miró, 1782-1792.* New Orleans, 1940.

Duffy, John (ed.). *The Rudolph Matas History of Medicine in Louisiana.* 2 vols. Baton Rouge, 1958, 1962.

Fortier, Alcée. *A History of Louisiana.* 4 vols. New York & Paris, 1904.

Gayarré, Charles Etienne Arthur. *History of Louisiana, the French Domination.* 2 vols. New York, 1866.

——————————. *History of Louisiana, the Spanish Domination.* New York, 1854.

Giraud, Marcel. *Histoire de la Louisiane Française.* 3 vols. Paris, 1953, 1958, 1966.

Holmes, Jack D. L. *Gayoso, the Life of a Spanish Governor in the Mississippi Valley, 1789-1799.* Baton Rouge, 1965; reprinted Gloucester, Mass., 1968.

———————————. *The Wax Tree: Louisiana's Forgotten Product,* with Raymond J. Martinez, *The Story of Spanish Moss: What it Is and How it Grows.* New Orleans, 1968.

Martin, François Xavier. *The History of Louisiana, from the Earliest Period.* rev. ed. New Orleans, 1882.

Whitaker, Arthur Preston. *The Mississippi Question, 1795-1803.* New York, 1934.

SECONDARY SOURCES. ARTICLES

Carrigan, Jo Ann. "The Pestilence of 1796—New Orleans' First Officially Recorded Yellow Fever Epidemic." *McNeese Review* (Lake Charles, La.), XIII (1962), 27-36.

Cruzat, Heloise H. "The Ursulines of Louisiana." *Louisiana Historical Quarterly,* II, No. 1 (January, 1919), 5-23.

Hatcher, Mattie Austin. "The Louisiana Background of the Colonization of Texas. 1763-1803." *Southwestern Historical Quarterly,* XXIV, No. 3, (January, 1921), 169-94.

Holmes, Jack D. L. "Andrés Almonester y Roxas: Saint or Scoundrel?" *Louisiana Studies,* VII, No. 1 (Spring, 1968), 47-64.

———————————. "*Dramatis Personae* in Spanish Louisiana." *Louisiana Studies,* VI, No. 2 (Summer, 1967), 149-85.

———————————. "Medical Practice in the Lower Mississippi Valley During the Spanish Period. 1769-1803." *The Alabama Journal of Medical Sciences,* I, No. 3 (July, 1964), 332-38.

Wood, Minter. "Life in New Orleans in the Spanish Period." *Louisiana Historical Quarterly,* XXII, No. 3 (July, 1939), 642-709.

Bibliography

GENERAL REFERENCES

Page

28 Stanley S. Arthur —
OLD NEW ORLEANS

32 Hamilton W. Mabie —
FOOTPRINTS OF FOUR CENTURIES

41 Raymond J. Martinez —
THE STORY OF THE RIVER FRONT AT NEW ORLEANS

45 Henry Rightor —
STANDARD HISTORY OF NEW ORLEANS

46 The Duke of Saint-Simon —
MEMOIRS OF LOUIS XIV AND HIS REGENCY

49 Jack D. L. Holmes —
GAYOSO, THE LIFE OF A SPANISH GOVERNOR IN THE MISSISSIPPI VALLEY

36 Raymond J. Martinez —
THE STORY OF THE RIVER FRONT AT NEW ORLEANS

88 Dr. Albert E. Fossier —
NEW ORLEANS, THE GLAMOROUS PERIOD 1800-1840

120 Raymond J. Martinez —
THE STORY OF THE RIVER FRONT AT NEW ORLEANS

130 George P. Meade —
SUGAR, ITS IMPORTANCE IN FOOD PROCESSING HISTORY

129 George Reasons & Sam Patrick —
THEY HAD A DREAM

132 Raymond J. Martinez —
THE STORY OF MOLASSES

138 P. A. Campomier —
STATEMENT OF THE SUGAR CROP MADE IN LOUISIANA

Visit us at *www.quaintpress.com*.

www.ingramcontent.com/pod-product-compliance
Lightning Source LLC
Chambersburg PA
CBHW071721090426
42738CB00009B/1844